Strategies for Celebrating Life in the Face of Illness

EDMUND J. FANTINO, Ph.D.

Performance Management Publications (PMP)

Performance Management Publications (PMP)
3353 Peachtree Road NE, Suite 920
Atlanta, GA 30326
678.904.6140

ISBN-10: 0-937100-16-1

ISBN-13: 978-0-937100-16-5

Printed in the United States of America by ViaTech Publishing Solutions

2 3 4 5 6 7

Lisa Smith, Art Director (cover and text design)
Gail Snyder, Editor

PMP is a division of Aubrey Daniels International, Inc.
PMP books are available at special discounts for bulk purchases by
corporations, institutions, and other organizations. For more information,
please call 678.904.6140, ext. 131 or e-mail lglass@aubreydaniels.com

additional praise for
Behaving Well

This gem of a book shows how powerful tools of judgement and decision making may empower us to experience richer lives.

– Craig R. M. McKenzie

Professor of Management and Strategy
Rady School of Management
Professor of Psychology, University of California,
San Diego

As a researcher in addiction I was struck by the relevance and usefulness of this book for better arranging our lives.

– Jed E. Rose, Ph.D.

Director, Center for Nicotine &
Smoking Cessation Research
Duke University Medical Center

Edmund Fantino is a highly respected behavioral psychologist who has become a 19-year survivor of metastatic cancer by putting classic principles of behavior into concrete action. The techniques of self-control he implemented extend beyond his own example of managing a major health problem, and provide a guide to self-management in general.

– Ben Williams

author of *Surviving Terminal Cancer:*
Clinical Trials, Drug Cocktails, &
Other Treatments Your Oncologist Won't Tell You About

foreword

Aubrey C. Daniels, Ph.D.
AUBREY DANIELS INTERNATIONAL

As a behavioral scientist, I have devoted my career to teaching and enabling people to use the science of applied behavior analysis to improve their lives in every arena of performance, with a primary emphasis on making the workplace a reinforcing and productive enterprise. Having this science and its practical use as a lifelong passion, I am of course aware of the many contributions that Dr. Edmund J. Fantino, the author of this book, has made to the behavior analytic community. From an esteemed Harvard University student to his position today as a distinguished professor of psychology and neurosciences at the University of San Diego, California, Edmund has become a world-renowned expert and prolifically published writer on the topic of human behavior and its many intricacies.

Ironically, decades ago, in an article called "The Nurturing of a Behavior Analyst," Edmund wrote of his early exposure to the science within the confines of

Harvard's Pigeon Laboratory: "I had little interest in behavior analysis, regarding it as too restrictive and narrow to deal with the rich tapestry of human behavior." Two and a half years later, Edmund confesses, he was a "committed behaviorist." I am very grateful (as I'm sure his students and colleagues are) for this transformation and the many positive works that followed.

In this book, which chronicles his life after the grim diagnosis of incurable cancer, he shares his personal journey while giving readers the gift of the lessons he learned. These lessons are not limited to the circumstances that Edmund has faced, but are instrumental for not only surviving, but thriving, when faced with challenges that at times seem too difficult to withstand. Edmund also has the warmth and talent to share his story in terms that scientists and non-scientists can comprehend and use. A Buddhist monk once said, "To know and not to do is not yet to know." My own translation of that quote is, "Walk the talk." Surely, the experiences in this book show that Edmund has done so by using his scientific knowledge to deal (and to deal bravely and brilliantly) with the rich tapestry of his own human behavior.

Edmund concluded the aforementioned article with an explanation of his devotion to the science he once thought lacking: "I had come to the conclusion that behavior analysis had the potential for answering the largest questions about human behavior, a position I hold to this day. I have never looked back."

I am very glad that he didn't, and I'm sure the readers of this book will agree.

−ACD

introduction

This is a remarkable personal account written by one of America's leading experts on human behavior, Edmund J. Fantino, Ph.D. In telling his story of dealing with advanced prostate cancer, Fantino candidly reveals the specific aspects of the disease while conveying a larger lesson. The details of coping with a grim diagnosis and the management of treatment form the core of this book, and are in themselves of great value, but the essence of this narrative is larger than one man's personal discoveries about a terrifying disease. The specific lesson is how he managed one of life's most distressing events while still managing to live his life. The larger lesson is a universal blueprint for building constructive behaviors that enable us to live our lives to the fullest.

From the day that we are born, we travel toward the ultimate destiny of our own demise. Yet, most of us assume that this seemingly far-distant ultimatum is prefaced by odds-beating decades filled with the immediate rewards of living. Love, family, career, adventure: these are the types of life events that keep us going, often in full throttle, absent of much contemplation about the final consequences that await us. Because of that full throttle approach, many of us rarely, if ever, reconsider our routines or seriously strive for changes that would enable us to live in the way we want. The author received a challenge that forced him to not only contemplate but activate such changes, and he shares his findings with us.

Fantino, Distinguished Professor of Psychology, and of the Neurosciences Group, University of California, San Diego, understood only too well the statistical realities that he faced when given his diagnosis. The prognosis was less than a year to live. Dr. Fantino, while a scientist, is as vulnerable to the same fears elicited by such a harsh diagnosis as any of us. His experiences in life, including his training as a scientist, provided him the ability to consider his illness objectively and somewhat dispassionately, including the wherewithal to explore optional approaches to his doctors' recommendations. He has written this book eighteen years after that first, dire diagnosis and provides a thoughtful, careful analysis of how he beat incredible odds.

At one point in his successful life, Fantino set the goal to write a book about how humans deal with adversity and stress, long before his illness appeared. He has bravely combined a scientific approach with one of open-mindedly accessing the possibilities of alternative theories not necessarily supported by accepted scientific practice; nevertheless, with sufficient data to make the exploration worthwhile. The book that he once planned has become a reality, based on personal experience tied to data-based expertise. Along the way, he introduces us to his loving companion and soul mate on this journey, his beloved wife, Stephanie, whom we recognize as having a very large degree of courage to see him through years of pain and discovery. Her optimism and strength infuses his tale and we learn, through few but well-chosen words, what it means to love another well.

Fantino's story is at first glance a very personal one of dealing with disease and the horrifying prognosis of eminent death. However, Fantino, forced into seemingly no-win choices, quickly discovers that death is a deadline to be filled, as all of life, with goals along the way—and in setting those goals, he begins a journey of both self-discovery and of hope.

The author's message is that despite our best efforts, our lives will not turn out exactly as we had planned. As creatures responsive to the scientific laws of behavior, we tend to manage our lives as though our long-term consequences are just that—and then something comes along and tells us that our long term is rather nearby. In a stressful world, even given the best of efforts, we cannot control the events that will alter our lives or the lives of those we love. We can, however, arrange conditions to help us take charge of our emotional reactions and our overt behavior in ways that might possibly alter the future. Since control over traumatic events is at best limited, most importantly, we can take charge of how we arrange conditions that affect our enjoyment of the present, as much as we possibly can.

If you face terrifying news or if you simply want to embrace the life you have, read this book and consider its teaching points. All too often, those who face difficult dilemmas requiring self-management do not have the tools to do so—even if they have the hope that Fantino describes. The author's suggestions, while highly applicable to those facing the frightening prospect of life-threatening disease, are equally relevant to those who want to change their approach to stressful and unfulfilling life styles by directing their energies toward positive change. Fortunately for all of us, the behaviors consistent with optimism and hope can be learned and self-managed. This is not a tale of dying, but of learning to live fully *life* in the best sense of the word.

contents

Foreword . . . . *vii*

Introduction . . . . *ix*

1 The Other Shoe Drops **1**

2 Halloween Horrors **5**

3 Fighting Back **19**

4 Life Begins at Eighty **43**

5 Self-Control **69**

6 Know Thyself **97**

7 Additional Five-Year Plans **109**

About the Author *119*

About ADI *120*

Register Your Book *122*

the other shoe drops

We all have plans. Short-term plans such as beginning this book, intermediate plans such as where to vacation next summer, and longer-term plans such as those surrounding retirement. These plans may take on a greater urgency when we learn that we have a fatal illness. This has happened to me and the experience has taught me how to better enjoy life. I'm convinced that the lessons I've learned may be useful to all of us mortals, not just those of us with reduced life expectancies.

Until I received some shocking health news, I considered myself an uncommonly lucky man. I recall walking along a beach in Kauai with my wife Stephanie one balmy afternoon, inwardly counting my blessings: A loving, intelligent, beautiful wife; marvelous, healthy children; an exciting and reasonably successful career as an experimental psychologist; a lovely home in beautiful Del Mar, California; and financial security. It almost didn't seem fair that life was so good to me. Moreover, given my parents' longevity and our family's own sound health habits, it appeared likely that Stephanie and I could enjoy life and traveling for scores of years to come. I mused, when will the other shoe drop? In other words, when would we be tested with a dose of life's sterner medicine?

As I so mused, of course, I had no way of knowing that prostate cancer was already spreading within me. The shoe was silently slipping. In the month of October 1988, I went from an individual confident of his health and likely longevity to one confronting an early demise. But before I recount some of the low lights of that October, I preview the overall plan of my story.

Part of my story is my reaction, and those of my family and friends, to my changed outlook. At the time, though devastated, I did not realize how fully my behavior, including my emotions and motivation, were affected by this changed outlook. With Stephanie's help, and that of others, I gradually adopted a more constructive attitude. I began applying the psychological principles I have spent my life researching to my situation. I adopted alternative health strategies, since conventional medicine had only a modest amount to offer me. Soon I was enjoying life more than I had been before learning that I had an incurable cancer.

But surely it should not have taken a death sentence to cause me to rearrange my life and fully appreciate it. Perhaps my experience may be a lesson to others, including those in sound health, that we must better appreciate what life, too short for most of us, offers. That's one reason for writing my story. A second is that I have been urged to do so by friends, advisors, and colleagues. Most importantly, I have always been convinced that behavioral principles can enrich all of our lives. I had always thought that upon retirement I might write a popular account on the application of these principles to improving our everyday lives. But I no longer have the luxury of delay. More-

over, I now have a greater appreciation of the power of
these behavioral principles. So my aim is nothing less
than to help you gain better control of your behavior and
to redirect it the way you want for a richer and more productive life.

The book includes discussion of the most central behavioral principles and their applications. The principles are
simple ones. My task is convincing you that such simple
principles can make a profound change in your life. Your
task will be to try them and reap the benefits. I'll introduce the principles in the framework of relating my own
battle with prostate cancer. In the next chapter the
emphasis will be on my confrontation with cancer. The
principles of behavior will be encountered as my efforts
evolved to right my life in the face of an incurable disease. The story is all too true and I hope its ending is
many chapters away. But we perhaps should begin with
the low point: my experiences leading up to an operation
on Halloween, 1988.

 tips for living ────────────────────────

Life has a way of coming at us fast. So here are some tips
for living that I learned shortly after discovering what it
meant to be a cancer patient. Some of the steps may apply
more specifically to dealing with serious illness, but many of
them can be applied to simply coping skillfully with the problems that life throws at us. I will provide a list of these life
tips at the end of each chapter. Some are easy to say, yet
harder to do, but as we progress through this book, I will
provide more details about how to manage change using the

tools of behavior analysis. Let's begin where I began with a gradual understanding of the initial steps for helping myself.

WHETHER YOU HAVE plans for a short-term, interim, or long-term goal, take a first step, no matter how small. Get started now! Write the goal down in terms of when, what, where, who, and how. Look at it. Think about it. What will it take for you to do it? As we progress through this book, you will get more pointers on how to turn a goal statement into something of real, directional, and life-changing value.

STOP TO ENJOY THE EXPERIENCE we call life: stand still; breathe in and out slowly to calm yourself. Gaze at the sky and your surroundings for a few minutes every day. Do this as part of your physical fitness plan.

CHECK YOUR OUTLOOK—optimistic, pessimistic, calm, anxious, angry. Write down when, where, who, and what leads to more positive feelings and to less positive feelings. Don't worry if you are not exactly right in every detail; just get a take on how the world affects you and how you tend to respond. Find one or two things you can do that make you feel better when experiencing negative emotions. Avoid surroundings, experiences, and people that bring you down. We will explore the scientific basis for the importance of understanding the environmental events that affect our behavior, including our emotions, when we discuss stimulus control.

halloween horrors

Life could not be better. Or so I had thought. Admittedly, there were frustrations, annoyances, occasional stresses when things didn't go right. In my case problems usually revolved around having too little time to accomplish all my objectives. I love my work. But between conducting laboratory research (on how we learn, what motivates us, the analysis of decision-making and self-control), supervising student research, teaching classes and attending to a number of administrative tasks at my university (UCSD, the University of California, San Diego), I am busy. Moreover, over the past forty-odd years I have had the good fortune to receive continuous funding for my research from either the National Institute of Mental Health (NIMH) or the National Science Foundation (NSF). But in order to receive this critical support it is necessary to submit periodic grant renewal applications and progress reports which are extremely labor-intensive. In the fall of 1988 I was also a member of an NSF review panel that evaluates over one hundred proposals each year and advises on their acceptability. This unpaid work requires about a month of effort before each of two meetings per year in Washington, D.C. I was also in the first year of a four-year term as Editor of the major journal in my field, the *Journal of the Experimental Analysis of Behavior*. How does one have time for all this and also for one's family and for pursuing other interests (in my case then, running, hiking, bicycling, reading fiction, camping, and traveling)? The answer, of course, involves careful planning and efficient management of one's time. Equally obvious, however, these plans don't always work out. Hence the occasional stress.

To summarize my outlook in the fall of 1988, I was a happy individual who enjoyed almost everything he did but who often felt stressed because he had trouble doing all he was committed to do. I was convinced I was doing my best. I now know I was selling myself short. It took some dreadful news to make me aware that life should have been even better.

This news began with an annual checkup. My doctor at the Scripps Clinic in La Jolla noticed an enlarged prostate with a standard rectal exam and referred me to a Scripps urologist. He also ordered a large battery of standard tests, since I was approaching fifty years, to assess my general health and fitness. On October 4 I spent most of the day at Scripps Clinic reading manuscripts and grant proposals while undergoing the medical tests. My appointment with the urologist was to come at the end of the day. I was not much concerned. Prostate cancer doesn't often strike forty-nine-year-olds with good health habits, I reasoned. Moreover, I didn't fully appreciate how deadly the disease often is. As the day wore on I became less concerned: All my tests were excellent, nurses and a patient admired my treadmill performance (I was a long-

distance runner) and the doctor who performed my sig-
moidoscopy (intense intestinal exam) not only found no
problem but said my prostate gland felt fine. I felt that
the urology appointment was almost unnecessary.

The urologist, however, did not like the feel of my
prostate gland and ordered a biopsy. On Friday morning
October 7, I was shocked to learn I had prostate cancer.
But I still didn't fully appreciate the life-threatening potential. I was more concerned with possible side effects of
the expected treatment, such as impotence. Meanwhile,
guests were coming for dinner and our family was going
camping for the weekend so there was not much time to
worry. But worry I did as I looked forward to a week of
further tests (including a bone scan and CAT-scan) to
determine if the cancer had spread beyond the prostate,
in which case the disease is incurable. I would learn the
result the following Friday: If the tests were negative, surgery to remove the prostate would be scheduled. If the
results were positive...but I did not permit myself to contemplate this darker possibility. Meanwhile I had my tests
and continued with my work, feeling anxious all the while.
Stephanie spent time in the UCSD Biomedical Library
learning about prostate cancer and its treatment options.

On Friday morning we arose early and went to our
appointment at Scripps Clinic. When the nurse asked how
I was that morning I replied, "scared," and was only half
joking. But the news was good! The tests revealed no
spread beyond the prostate and my urologist suggested that
a radical prostectomy (removal of the prostate gland and
surrounding lymph nodes) could well result in a complete
cure. We were elated. I reflected that it would have been

difficult for me to believe two weeks earlier that I would be elated with a diagnosis of prostate cancer. Compared to the possibility of the immediately preceding days, however, this seemed a new lease on life. We scheduled the surgery for the morning of October 31 after I returned from the NSF review panel meeting in Washington D.C.; during these two weeks, I was also to donate the blood needed for the long operation.

Despite my renewed optimism, I knew there were still potential pitfalls, in addition to the delicacy of the surgery itself and some potentially serious side effects. For one, even if the operation was apparently successful there was some chance that the cancer had spread undetected beyond the prostate area and that this metastasis would become evident in later years. Second, I might get news of this metastasis as early as October 31. The first stage of the operation involved removal and biopsy of the surrounding lymph glands. If there was already substantial spread to the lymph system (undetected by the negative CAT scan), the operation would go no further and I would be facing an incurable stage of prostate cancer. So my optimism had its bounds.

I returned from Washington D.C. on Friday night, October 28. We spent the weekend on a camping trip with friends from a local branch of the Sierra Club. This was a Halloween-oriented weekend of the Focus on Youth section of the Club and an outing populated with happy, energetic children. It provided a world of incentive to live and see our children grow. Our own daughters, Ramona and Marin, were eight and four at that time. They knew of my condition but we didn't dwell on its life-threatening aspect.

The weekend, in the beautiful Laguna Mountains, less than a two-hour drive east of San Diego, afforded a chance to enjoy our children and others, to celebrate Halloween a bit early, and to do some hiking. It also gave us a chance to tell our tale on Sunday of the next day's operation (two of our group are nurses). We received much-welcomed support from our camping friends.

On Monday morning we made the ten-minute drive to Scripps armed with enough books and cassette tapes to get me through what was to be a stay of several days. In the early afternoon, I was anesthetized expecting to awaken in late afternoon.

My first hint that something was wrong came when I opened my eyes in the recovery room. The clock said 2:30, earlier than I had expected. I asked a nurse if my prostate had been removed but she said I would have to ask my doctor. I was soon back in my room and Stephanie broke the news to me: The operation ended after the lymph nodes were examined. There was significant involvement in nodes on either side of the prostate. Somehow I felt it was my fault and I apologized to Stephanie. I was emotionally stunned and kept thinking of how I had let my family down. In the subsequent evening, I imagined my situation to be even worse than it objectively was. My morphine-induced sleep was fitful. I awoke repeatedly with the conviction that I had only months to live, whereas I could probably count on at least a year.

In other words, I was totally unprepared, at least emotionally, for my new outlook. I had several needs: First, to come to terms with, and understand, this new situation; second, to take a constructive approach to my disease by trying to learn what I could about treatment options, and third, whatever my options, to structure my life, both my actions and emotions, to make the best of my situation. Nothing could be gained by self-pity or by dwelling upon how unfair or unlucky my plight. At the very least I owed it to my family to maintain a positive attitude.

How to achieve these goals? Coming to terms with my drastically shortened life expectancy was relatively simple intellectually. Nothing could be done about it by bemoaning this change. Instead, my energies had to be directed at finding out what I **could do** and what I **should do**. And the very first thing that required doing was to learn more about my disease and treatment. This posed an immediate dilemma. The articles in the medical journals about metastasized prostate cancer are rather depressing in terms of survival rates, the discomfort involved as the disease spreads (especially to the bones), and the side effects of treatment (including impotence, severe hot flashes, severe edema, incontinence and others, depending upon the treatment). How to become better informed and develop a positive emotional outlook at the same time?

We decided that Stephanie would bear the brunt of the stress-inducing research and I would learn the principal findings. If a study were particularly important, such as one purporting to demonstrate good results with radiation of a large area around the prostate, given us to read by a radiologist at Scripps, I too read it. Otherwise, I was spared the graphic details. In addition to reading in the current oncology and urology journals, we consulted several experts around the country, either directly by telephone or indirectly through friends at other universities. In this way we obtained a wealth of information about the current status of treatment for metastasized prostate cancer. Unfortunately, much of the advice was contradictory and none of it suggested the possibility of a cure. There were two encouraging straws to grasp, however, and soon they became three. When you are adrift at sea, three slender straws are immensely better than none. Also, when you are busy gathering the straws you don't have as much time to feel sorry for yourself or to ask, "Why me?" And the time, attention, and compassion shown by our medical advisers was heartening. For example, one oncologist, then at Sloan-Kettering in New York City, spent a half-hour reviewing literature and dispensing advice for us in a telephone conference without charging us. Our radiologist at Scripps Clinic spent half a morning with us, occasionally darting out to meet other patients, going over the rationale and methodology of radiation treatment in great detail. Our impression of the medical community was enhanced by our experience.

After two weeks of intensive research, what had we found out and what were the straws of hope in the winds of despair?

In terms of statistics, it was doubtful that I would live five years. The five-year survival rate refers to the percentage of people still alive in five years' time. In the case of metastasized prostate cancer this rate was 29 percent at the time of my diagnosis. In other words only twenty-nine people in one hundred with my condition remained alive five years later. Of the treatment options, the most promising was antihormonal treatment (chemical castration) which sharply reduced or eliminated the production of male hormones. This is effective because prostate cancer thrives on male hormones. But, while this treatment stalls and sometimes reverses the advance of symptoms in most patients, its effectiveness is generally temporary (typically, two years, with large differences between individual cases). Why temporary? It is believed that not all prostate cancer cells are hormone-dependent, though these are thought to be the most rapidly spreading. In addition, there are hormone-independent cells, for which there is no effective treatment. Eventually, these prove fatal.

There were two major decisions we had to make, each involving issues about which there was controversy within the medical profession. First, should I undergo radiation of the prostate even though the cancer had spread beyond and, if so, should the radiation be restricted to the prostate area, or should it take in a large area of the surrounding pelvis to include significant amounts of the lymphatic system? Second, should we begin the anti-hormone treatment now or wait until I developed symptoms (for example bone involvement)?

Almost complete agreement was registered on the possibility of aggressive radiation therapy. We were warned by most of our advisers that the danger of side effects or morbidity likely to result from such therapy far outweighed the almost intangible possibility of a positive outcome. There was less agreement concerning whether a more modest radiation therapy was worth risking. Those who argued against it, and they were in the majority, used analogies such as closing the barn door after the horse has escaped, to illustrate their point that since the cancer had already spread beyond the prostate there was no reason to risk serious side effects by attempting to kill the cancer cells within the prostate. And even with radiation restricted to the prostate, some possibility remained that impotence, incontinence, or severe edema could result. The edema, facilitated by the previous removal of the lymph nodes, potentially might be serious enough to make even walking difficult, a particular worry for an inveterate runner and walker. The two or three who argued for restricted radiation suggested that the risk of side effects with radiation of the prostate alone was probably minimal in someone my age and that there was the possibility of benefit. With production of cancer cells by the prostate ("the mother tumor" as one urologist phrased it) eliminated, perhaps the cancer would spread less rapidly.

Even more controversial was the question of whether to begin antihormonal therapy. Some argued that it should begin immediately in order to slow down the spread at once and conceivably to reduce the development (but not the advance) of even the hormone-independent cancer cells (which may develop initially from the hormone-dependent cells in a process that may resemble mutation). Others argued that there was no evidence that early pre-symptomatic treatment added to longevity. In other words, people who underwent treatment at the first opportunity did not survive any longer, on the average, than those who weren't treated until they developed symptoms. Moreover, the treatment would severely reduce my quality of life, in that it would likely produce impotence and severe hot flashes that some patients regarded as unbearable and embarrassing. At least two advisers, a urologist at UCSD and a well-known prostate cancer and cancer researcher at the National Institutes of Health (NIH) suggested that despite the absence of solid supporting data, the efficacy of early antihormone treatment might yet be demonstrated.

Based on all this advice and on our own (mostly Stephanie's) readings in medical journals, we had to arrive at a decision. Moreover, there was some urgency in this. At least we received the clear impression from several of the people we consulted that my cancer was probably fairly aggressive. Some years later one of those doctors admitted that, at the time, he didn't think I would last more than one year. The UCSD urologist and the NIH researcher had recommended combining early antihormonal treatment with local radiation of the prostate and we were leaning toward this approach. But before indicating what we actually did, I need to relate a simultaneously occurring development concerning those straws of hope I mentioned earlier.

First of all, Stephanie was struck by the gross discrepancies across different articles on survival prospects in prostate cancer patients. In the language of psychological statistics, the data would be termed *highly variable*. At the positive end, some groups of patients survived five years without symptoms; that is, they did much better than the 29 percent, five-year survival rate would suggest. At the low end, in one study just about all the patients in my situation were dead or doing poorly in just twelve months time. This was the kind of study Stephanie and I agreed would derive me no great benefit to read in graphic detail.

Now, there was nothing obviously different about those

groups of patients who did relatively well and those who did not. What this suggested to us is that there are unknown factors influencing the progression of the disease. Some, presumably, are related to the types and distributions of cancer cells and other factors over which we may have little control. But others may involve variables that we can influence. In particular, it may be that by strengthening our immune systems we can slow the progression of the disease. So we explored methods that might bolster the immune system. And, incidentally, we also realized that we might weaken the immune system with radiation therapy, owing to likely damaging affected bone marrow in the radiated area. Our radiologist at Scripps was very helpful in estimating the potential extent of such damage.

In other words, the first straw we grasped is that patients differ radically in how they respond to spreading prostate cancer. This gave us a role in trying to put me at the long-lived end of the distribution. The mere act of taking on such a role may be therapeutic. Some behavioral studies suggest that stress is dealt with more effectively when the subject has relatively more control over his situation. (A striking example of this research is discussed in the next chapter.) The possibility exists that the relatively simple action of designing an alternative treatment program might reduce stress and bolster the immune system almost independent of the merits of the specific components making up that program.

We decided to incorporate two major changes in life style that we felt might plausibly bolster the immune system. These are our second and third straws, and almost twenty years later we cling to them still. While in the gloom of that hospital room on Halloween Monday, Stephanie mentioned "going on a macrobiotic diet." She had read some case studies of cancer patients responding well to this diet, particularly patients with metastasized prostate cancer. There was no hard evidence, of course, and as one skeptical doctor in the literature noted, "there never will be." But what did we have to lose? On that Friday, we began a transition to a full macrobiotic diet. Later I will discuss the nature of the diet, its strengths and weaknesses from the point of view of being a realistic and practical adjustment in life style for most people, and some of the indirect and anecdotal evidence for why it is worth taking seriously. The other change involved adopting a battery of Kundalini Yoga exercises designed to strengthen the immune system. Indeed both the yoga exercises and the macrobiotic diet have similar explicit goals: strengthen the immune system and eliminate toxic waste products that have accumulated in our bodies. These seemed like commendable goals in any event. Moreover, neither the diet nor the exercises are invasive or likely to produce any harm. Both require expenditure of time and change in life style. As I indicated earlier, time was a precious commodity for me even before I found I had much less left of it; but we regarded the time spent on these diet and exercise regimes as an investment in the future. And, I think it's critical to be convinced one has a future and that one can affect its course. In the weeks succeeding my operation I sometimes lost this simple insight. I'll start the next chapter with a good example of this; an example which puts me in a dim light, I'm afraid. But the story will also launch us into a discussion of some of the psychological principles illustrated by this tale thus far. Understanding these principles will help us better understand ourselves and place us in a better position to cope effectively with the stresses that life sometimes imposes on us.

 tips for living ————————————————

BALANCE THE PORTIONS ON YOUR PLATE including work, family, self, and community. *Balance* is easy to say but difficult to do. You might find that your focus is currently exactly as you like it. For example, your idea of balance may be a plate half full of family and half full of other things. *Balance* is a word subject to personal interpretation. Some of us, however, never really stop and seriously think about what we are currently doing and if it is really what we want. There is no time like the present to do so. For example, if you do for others and rarely for yourself, take that bit of knowledge and consider how to focus on yourself once in a while by taking more time for activities that you enjoy.

LIMIT YOUR COMMITMENTS to doable and primarily enjoyable activities. You don't have to say "yes" to be OK, and you will probably find this one step alone very liberating.

PLAN TIME TO LIVE IN THE MOMENT: watch your children, play with your pets, and take a walk with your spouse. We sometimes have difficulty acknowledging and appreciating special moments, but they are available to us all the time.

ENJOY NATURE AND THE POSITIVES that life has already given you. This is about counting good things. It matters.

RESEARCH OPTIONS PRIOR TO TOUGH DECISIONS. In the case of illness, an informed decision can reduce stress. Share information with your doctor and seek out physicians who are willing to talk to you about the pros and cons of alternative treatments. Do not be afraid to ask questions. Be sure to listen with receptivity to what you are told.

STOP NEGATIVE THOUGHTS with counteractive constructive actions. This could mean simply getting up and moving to another location, organizing a drawer, or throwing a Frisbee for the dog. Thought stoppage is a therapy technique that has had good effect on people who are plagued with sad, repetitive, or destructive thoughts. Tell yourself to "stop" and then move on to a distracting activity, ideally an activity that involves sound or competing attention to take your mind off your current negative thoughts. This kind of distraction must be dramatic at times but is essential for many of us who are consumed by worry or negative thoughts about our ability to handle challenges or to make changes.

FACE REALITY and feed yourself with good news. That includes good news from sports, community, and other sources, not just good news about you or those you love.

DEVELOP HABITS that boost your immune system. These include exercise, yoga, meditation of all sorts, and healthy eating.

fighting back

We hear so much about the importance of maintaining a positive attitude. This is good advice as we will see. But, as with much good advice, this advice is not always easy to follow especially when your world appears to be tumbling about you. How do you maintain a positive attitude when contemplating that you are unlikely to see your children become teenagers, much less reach college age? Speaking of which, what of all those college tuition fees? Each day was replete with harsh realities that discouraged the kind of optimistic outlook that would be helpful to combat these realities.

Stephanie related to me studies of cancer patients showing that those who put great faith in medical statistics regarding survival outlook in metastasized cancer were more likely to die sooner than those with less appreciation of these generally gloomy statistics. This was a thinly veiled warning to me, a great believer in statistics and logic. And while I took steps to combat the kind of pessimism that might help fulfill the statistical facts, I sometimes caught myself slipping backward down the slick slope of negativity and self-pity.

A good example occurred in my dentist's office. We were discussing my eventual need for a gold crown on one of my molars. I was more vociferous in advocating delay than was usual for me. I even said that I saw no reason for great expense if the problem would not become serious within the year since that might be as long as I could expect to be alive. Some time later I was horrified at this reaction. How could such self-defeating statements co-exist with other aspects of my behavior which were constructive and as optimistic as the realities of my situation permitted? As a psychologist, I should not have been surprised. Our behaviors are not generally consistent. We can be constructive in some situations, destructive in others; show impulsivity in some contexts, self-control in others; honest in some cases (for instance, in dealing with friends), dishonest in some others (for instance, in reporting expenses or occasional wages to impersonal organizations, such as the IRS). Indeed the situational determinants of human behavior are known to be powerful.

Most of us are familiar with the phrase *self-fulfilling prophecy*. Briefly, if we believe something strongly enough it may become more likely. In this case the goal is to believe one can be one of the survivors (at least one of the 29 percent still alive after five years) and not one of the statistics (or the majority 71 percent who die along the way). Why should self-fulfilling prophecies occur in these cases? No one is sure, or at least on the basis of scientific evidence no one **should** be sure; however, we do have some good guesses. Again, the immune system is a likely participant. The stress associated with a negative attitude is likely to weaken the immune system and facilitate fulfillment of the negative outcome.

In addition, one's attitude will affect how others react to you. And their reactions in turn are likely to affect your attitude. A person with a highly negative, self-pitying attitude is likely to generate a pessimistic reaction in others. In some cases, the reaction will be one of avoidance, a reaction that can make the sufferer still more despondent.

The patient who acts like a non-survivor may be unconsciously labeled as such and be treated differently than one who acts more positively. How we are characterized by others can have a profound influence. One of my favorite examples involves a study done some years ago about being sane in insane places. As part of a psychological experiment, several individuals faked standard psychiatric symptoms in order to gain admittance to a psychiatric ward. They were successful. But as soon as they gained admittance they began behaving normally and insisted that they were fine. Hence they were being sane, that is behaving normally, in an insane place, the psychiatric ward. Was their sanity detected? Not by the psychiatric personnel who kept them incarcerated. Interestingly, their fellow patients, themselves legitimately diagnosed with abnormal behavior, detected the impostors' sanity. In a sense those detections provide an unintended control group in this situation. Specifically, the behavior of the impostors **was** discriminably different from that of the legitimate patients. However, given the psychiatric labels that the impostors carried with them from their diagnosis, this differential behavior was not perceived (or at least acknowledged) by the psychiatric staff, doctors, and nurses.

To the extent, then, that we may influence our health by our attitude and by others' resultant attitude toward us, we need a constructive positive outlook. A related lesson comes from studies showing on what days people are likely to die. A vast study of this subject has been conducted over the years by my colleague at UCSD, sociologist Dr. David Phillips. He has shown, for example, that people are **less likely** to die just before Christmas than on other days and that they are **more likely** to die on the day after Christmas than on other days. Together, these facts, along with others uncovered by Professor Phillips' painstaking statistical research, suggest that individuals may delay their deaths in order to live through an event that has great meaning or enjoyment for them and their loved ones. This suggests the importance of setting goals. In a sense, goals to live for (and until)!

But let us return to the vexing challenge of maintaining a positive attitude in the face of a grim prognosis. With respect to the medical situation confronting the patient, it is, of course, essential to learn as much as possible about the disease and its treatment, both within the framework of conventional medicine and alternative treatments. If the patient has a spouse or friend who can help, as I did, that person should undertake filtering the material so that grim and graphic details are transmitted only when necessary for intelligent decision making.

The patient should focus on what **can** be done in terms of fighting the disease and on what **can** be done in terms of enjoying life. The patient should set goals, regarding any behavioral and psychological adjustments for fighting the disease and goals regarding corresponding adjustments for ordering one's life. Unnecessary dross and tedium should be eliminated wherever possible. Let's discuss each of these suggestions in turn.

First, consult doctors and carefully consult the medical literature. A wealth of information is available on Web sites and libraries, especially university libraries. Best yet are the medical libraries of university medical schools. Moreover, many of these libraries have computer facilities to conduct literature searches on particular subjects. Begin with the disease (in my case prostate cancer) and then move on to searches involving particular tests (for example, the prostate specific antigen or PSA test), particular treatments (such as radiation or hormonal therapy) and ongoing clinical trials (generally involving experimental approaches). In a day or two, one can become something of an expert in the medical literature concerning one's particular ailment. Some of the medical literature can be difficult to understand, even for someone with a science background. Don't get bogged down in details nor feel obligated to carefully read all the available articles. Be guided by the summaries and aided by a medical dictionary. Also, as we will see later, gathering information includes receiving information you might have preferred not to encounter. While I was spared some of the grim and depressing details, Stephanie found her heart racing as she perused some of the articles.

Taking the initiative to gather information for dealing with life-threatening situations is not restricted to human health. A good friend and former student, named Alan, a professor at American University in Washington, D.C., offered to research prostate cancer for me in the marvelous libraries of the D.C. area. "I've got the whole Library of Congress at my disposal," he pointed out.

While we did not take him up on his offer, since we had excellent facilities in La Jolla, I do want to pass on some encouragement he gave us based on his own experience with his pet dog.

A veterinarian discovered that Alan's dog Merkin had cancer, determined in a radical mastectomy and subsequent biopsy. She was going to die soon, they were told, and nothing could be done. Alan and his wife Susan went to the National Library of Medicine and started learning about carcinoma in the female dog. They learned that cancer advances five times more rapidly in a dog than in humans and that Merkin's life expectancy was less than six months. Alan spent two days in the library, learning about possible treatments and then obtained the names of some veterinary oncologists and cancer researchers. He phoned experts in Texas, Florida, and even England. Ultimately, through a veterinarian in West Virginia, Alan got in touch with the veterinary facility associated with Sloan-Kettering Institute and obtained their protocol for administering a particular drug which had been tested with women who had developed breast cancer.

Alan (or rather Merkin's) regular veterinarian administered the chemotherapy protocol over several months. Merkin was cancer free for several years and died at a ripe old age of fourteen, by which time she had a reoccurrence of the tumor and heart problems. Alan's point in relating the story to me, of course, was to suggest that by using initiative, acquiring knowledge, and sparing no effort one may be able to radically improve one's chances for survival.

Information gathering with respect to alternative treatments was a bit less systematic, at least in our case. But there are several journals and magazines devoted to various alternative sources of health care, and additional advice may be found at health food stores, holistic health centers, and macrobiotic centers. Medical doctors can be a source of information, even about alternatives to standard accepted medical practice. We'll encounter personal examples when my own story resumes. Where cancer is the concern, good additional sources of information are the cancer telephone hot line (1-800-4-CANCER) which gives information regarding typical medical treatments for particular cancers and information about clinical trials for new (experimental) treatment. For information about alternative cancer treatments, a useful source is the Cancer Network, an umbrella organization which includes scores of alternative cancer treatment groups.

So, gathering information is not difficult if one has the time. When your life is at stake, finding the time is appropriate. But what to do with it is more difficult. I will relate my own choices but, clearly, another individual in my position might decide a different set of options is more suitable. But I do urge one approach: Seriously consider both standard and alternative treatment and attempt to combine them; do not adopt a relatively unproved alternative regimen without maintaining standard medical care as well. In other words, try to profit by what each has to offer. Be wary of any alternative treatment that advocates eliminating standard care. Be wary, as well, of medical doctors who appear to have their minds closed to even the possibility of effective alternative approaches. But remember also that, whereas your medical doctor has a level of competence ensured by his or her training, there is no similar guarantee for many alternative health practitioners. In the final analysis, you must sort through the information and advice and put together your own approach. Taking control, in this way, is already a step in the direction of improved health.

Is there evidence in the psychological literature that taking control of one's life helps to reduce stress? Is there evidence that reduction of stress helps to reduce illness? The answer to both questions appears to be "yes." Even when untoward events occur, their deleterious effects may be minimized if we have some control over them. In a cancer study, Sklar and Anisman (1979;1981) infected two groups of mice with tumor cells and subjected one group to electric shocks that the mice could escape. Mice in the other group received shocks at the same time as the first group. In other words, they received the same amount and distribution of shocks; but for the second group of mice, the shocks were inescapable. Mice in the inescapable group, that is those with no control over the aversive events, had significantly faster tumor growth than those who did have control.

Many other studies have shown that rats prefer to be subjected to predictable shocks rather than even more intense and more frequent unpredictable ones and that rats receiving unpredictable shocks are more prone to developing ulcers. Langer and Rodin (1976) conducted a famous study of an aged population in an institutional setting. They found that people who had been required to give up significant control over their lives, particularly involving making decisions, improved their lives and attitudes when they were given a renewed sense of personal responsibility. Their improvement was measured with self-reports and by ratings of the nurses on their floors.

Evidence that stress and illness are related comes from studies with healthy and ill samples of patients. For example, one study showed a direct relationship between stress, on the one hand, and infections and colds, on the other: Cohen, Tyrrell, and Smith (1991) found that the greater the recent and current psychological stress imposed on healthy human volunteers who were inoculated with a cold virus, the more likely they were to succumb to the cold (as measured in a set of questionnaires). Stress appears to produce weakening of the immune system. The relation between stress, quality of life, and the immune system in healthy individuals and in cancer patients has been reviewed by Andersen, Kiecolt-Glaser, and Glaser (1994).

The salubrious effects of having control of our lives may be related to our desire for choices. We seem to live in a society in which there are never enough options. Whereas much of this apparent desire for choices is no doubt foisted upon us by advertisers, there is evidence even in nonhuman species that choices are sometimes highly prized. Dr. A. Charles Catania of the University of Maryland has offered pigeons the following choice: One alternative leads to a single key which may be pecked to provide grain; the other alternative leads to two keys either of which may be pecked to produce grain. In either case, the amount of grain earned is exactly the same; yet the pigeons demonstrate a clear preference for the two-way option, a preference which Catania has termed one for freedom of choice.

Once we have obtained the information we need to make intelligent choices regarding treatment, we should take control of our lives in another fundamental way: we should set goals for what we can realistically experience and accomplish in the time we have left. This is a sound strategy whether we perceive that time to be a matter of months or a matter of seventy years. The shorter the expected time frame, of course, the more urgent the plan. We are all living a transitory, uncertain life. A few years ago a friend told me that we were all hanging on to life by a slender rope but that in my case the rope was more threadbare than most. Later that week, in response to another friend's query about my health, I related this observation to him. This friend, a cardiac surgeon, said that the observation didn't go far enough. From his medical perspective he would say all of us are hanging on to life by flimsy threads; by which he meant, of course, that none of us should take tomorrow for granted.

The lesson here is, that since our days are limited, let's make absolutely certain that we plan to spend them in the most fruitful manner possible. A great Roman once said, "Live each day as if it were your last." In spirit this is the way to live. In practice, however, it goes too far. Obviously, one must consider the likely reality of tomorrow and the possibility of many future days. I recall a short story I read in my youth in which the protagonist had a handsome fixed sum on which to live for the rest of his days. He calculated he would live to a reasonable age and decided to live as lavishly as possible during that time. Everything works out fine except he is still very much alive upon reaching the target age and is now penniless.

What then is a reasonable compromise between getting as much as possible out of life now and planning for a secure and fruitful future? First of all there are ways to redirect your life and energies so that you can get more out of life almost every day for as long as life lasts. While it took an incurable disease to teach me this lesson, I'm convinced that it applies to all of us. Second, I think five years is a reasonable time frame in which to consider goals and how to achieve them. In my case the five years was dictated by my prognosis: even making the assumption that I would live five more years could be regarded as optimistic; certainly, in terms of statistics the odds were against me.

The sense of urgency these odds instilled in me turned out to be my ally. As I set down my goals for the five years, I realized how much I wanted to do and how much I would enjoy doing them if given the opportunity. My goals regarding time to be spent with my family and watching my children grow seemed more precious than ever to me. My research ambitions were also more acute. There were questions I wanted answers to that could not wait beyond five years. As I noted earlier, there was a book I'd intended to write that required more immediate attention. I also made a list of the recreational interests I wanted to pursue: I must return to Sicily to see my sister and her family; I was intent upon traveling up the Stuart Highway through the red center of Australia from the south in Adelaide to the top end in Darwin; an avid reader of novels, I did not want to die without reading some of the great classics I had not yet had time to read.

Clearly, if I could order my life to accomplish most of these goals, I would be a happier person than I had been, my illness notwithstanding. I'll discuss briefly how this was accomplished in my case as it may be helpful for others thinking of redirecting their energies; but first, let me make a point I learned that was as significant as anything experience has taught me: Living on a five-year plan, that is under the assumption that five years is all I could reasonably expect, heightened my enjoyment of everything I did. I realized that the ideal life is one composed of renewable five-year plans. Even if I were not fortunate enough to start a second five-year period, I was enjoying life more than I ever had.

Perhaps I can illustrate my feelings with some lines from a poem by A.E. Housman that most of us read while in school. His narrator is a twenty-year old individual who is traveling the forest in mid-winter. After a marvelous description of a winter scene he notes the following:

> And take from seventy springs a score
> It leaves me only fifty more
> So about the woodlands I will go
> To see the cherry hung with snow

In other much more prosaic words, take advantage of what nature and life have to offer now. In the same vein, appreciate what you have. The trip to my office at UCSD

goes along a beautiful, even breathtaking, stretch of coast-
line before ascending through Torrey Pines State Reserve.
Since I learned of my illness, this view from my bus win-
dow every day is no longer taken for granted. Nor are the
sunsets over the Pacific Ocean.

Not all of our lives consist of wonderful moments and
scenes, however. Some activities that we don't enjoy must
be endured. In reassessing one's life one may find, as I
did, that there are activities that can be displaced in some
fashion. A key objective, in so far as it is possible, is to
minimize our least rewarding activities. Some activities
can simply be eliminated. For example, I stopped volun-
teering for (or agreeing to) various committee assignments at work and even in the community. At first I felt
a bit badly doing so; but, if I were serious about reducing
the stress that time-intensive activities produced, then I
had to make some hard choices. As far as committee work
at the university was concerned, I had done more than
my share over the years. Now I would say, "Sorry, no,"
unless the assignment particularly intrigued me. Similarly,
I made it clear that I would not serve as Chair of our
Department of Psychology. With respect to the community, I still wrote checks for our local environmental slow-
growth candidates and participated minimally in their
campaigns, but eliminated more ambitious help such as
door-to-door precinct walking on behalf of the candidates.
Instead we shifted our community involvement into activities that we felt were equally important but, for us, much
more enjoyable. As an example, we decided to devote
more time to the Sierra Club's Focus on Youth section.
We had been on many enjoyable outings with this group,

whose function is to get families camping at the deserts, lakes, and mountains of the San Diego area with the ultimate aim of instilling appreciation and respect for the outdoors in children. A tremendous amount of time is put into organizing, coordinating, and leading these activities. We felt that perhaps it was our time to take on some of this work. Thus, we decided to become leaders in the Sierra Club, a position that permits us to lead outings. Getting there proved half the fun!

Having the necessary knowledge and skills required to assume the responsibility for outings must be proved before becoming a Sierra Club leader. One requirement was a first-aid course, something every family should know. To satisfy a skills requirement, Stephanie and I decided to enroll in the Sierra Club's Basic Mountaineering Course (BMC). This ten-week course was one of the most enjoyable we have taken. The three-hour meetings each Tuesday evening were extremely informative and the four weekend outings were indispensable for acquiring wilderness know-how. Moreover, they were marvelous social occasions. They provided Stephanie and I with an opportunity we had had only once before: a weekend without our children. On one occasion soon after my operation, Stephanie and I had gone for a short, one-evening weekend in the Anza-Borrego Desert. Otherwise, in the eight-plus years since Ramona's birth, we had never been separated from our children. We thoroughly enjoyed our family outings but sometimes craved some time alone. This craving was not shared by our young family members, however. They were determined that we should be leaders, so they did not mind our joining these BMC outings without them.

The fourth outing, called "Snow Camp" took place in Mt. San Jacinto in early March. As its name implies, you learn to backpack and set up camp in the snow, and on this weekend we had snow! After an idyllic Saturday afternoon where ten of us picnicked in the pristine setting near our base camp, a blizzard began. The weekend tested us in terms of bitter cold, snow, winds, and altitude sickness. In one case, we temporarily lost a member of the group who had gone off to relieve himself. His tracks were so rapidly covered up that he wandered about for half an hour before we heard his cries. These tests taught us what to do in such situations and most importantly, gave us the confidence to believe we could deal with these circumstances should they arise in the future.

After taking an exam to pass the course we were then tested in a leadership-training backpack outing and soon were in a position to lead our own outings. Thus, to return to my earlier point, we rearranged our lives to combine community service with family activities we enjoyed immensely. At the same time, we eliminated other activities to make room for this new commitment.

Eliminating some committee work and administrative responsibilities at the university was not difficult and my academic life became less hectic and more enjoyable. There were other duties, however, that were as enjoyable and important to me as they were time consuming. Was my five-year plan to include continuing my work as editor and as a member of the NSF Grant Review Panel? In the interests of spending more time with my family, but not withdrawing from reviewing activities entirely, I decided to compromise: I resigned from the NSF panel, indicating

a willingness to serve again if asked and if in reasonable
health, when my term as editor ended in 1991. I would
complete my term as editor, health permitting. This decision to suspend my grant reviewing position freed up two
precious months a year.

What about that book I was planning to write on the
application of behavioral principles to everyday life? **This**
book. I decided this book would have to wait. Moreover, if,
after five years, I was alive and well enough to embark on
an enterprise such as writing, I would probably have more
of a story to tell. Thus, this book was relegated to a possible second five-year plan. I thought of it no more during
that five-year period.

With my work plans consolidated, I knew, given a reasonable (pain-free) physical condition, that I could accomplish my goals, that they were realistic, and that I could
do so with two important by-products (I avoid saying side
effects since that was becoming a dreaded term and one
too often in my vocabulary those days). First of all, I felt,
correctly as it turned out, that I could accomplish these
goals without undue stress from time pressures, especially
since much of the work could be done at my own pace.
Editing the journal, for example, while time consuming,
could be done **when** I wanted and **where** I wanted, including on the beach or while sitting on a bench at beautiful
Torrey Pines State Reserve. Second, it left me ample time
to spend with my family and on leisure pursuits.

Since I crave reading fiction, I made sure that I made
time for that. So I continued a strategy that had worked
for me since 1985 and works to this day. Back in the
autumn of 1984, I experienced one of the busiest periods

of my work life. I submitted, with a former student, an article to a journal called *The Behavioral and Brain Sciences*. The journal typically publishes three long articles in each of its four annual issues. Each article is followed by two dozen or so commentaries by experts in several different fields. These commentaries from a distinguished interdisciplinary group of scientists are often quite critical (as academics are wont to be). The original authors, though they cannot change the published version of their article, have the opportunity to follow with a response to the commentaries. The process of responding to some twenty-five very different, often complex and often critical commentaries can take time. And at the same time I had to submit a lengthy grant proposal, always a challenging and time-consuming task. All this coincided with the beginning of our school year. It added up to an extremely busy autumn consisting of eighty-hour work weeks. When the work was done, just before December 1, I decided to do as little as possible for five weeks and to spend a good deal of time reading. Ah, what a glorious five weeks I had!

Among my activities was rediscovering some favorite authors such as Graham Greene, the British novelist. It was also wonderful taking a trip to spend Christmas in New York City where we visited my parents. I decided that I had to continue reading novels; I wasn't going to wait until retirement to satisfy my craving for literature. I also knew that something like reading would likely take a back seat to the more pressing demands on my time once I was back at UCSD at the start of our winter quarter. Activities that occur only when I have some time often occur never at all.

I'm reminded of an experience having some photo-
graphs developed for a research publication. I dropped
them off at the photolab at Scripps Institute of
Oceanography (part of UCSD) and filled out the line
"when needed" with "as soon as possible" expecting to
have them ready in a day or two. A week later they were
still not ready, however. It developed that as soon as possible meant do this job only when all the jobs requested
for today are done. I was told that, in the future, I should
name a day!

If we are serious about undertaking an activity that we
are not required to perform, we had better make the time
for it. That's one reason scheduling exercise classes is an
effective method for making it more likely that you actually get some exercise. So, I scheduled times during the day
when I would do some reading; and not only when I was
preparing to go to sleep, since that might mean reading
only a page a night. By taking the bus to school instead
of driving, for example, I could fit in some reading. In
any event, I made the only New Year's resolution of my
life on January 1, 1985: I would read one novel a week
throughout the year. More precisely, since novels vary
greatly in length, I would read fifty-two novels that year.
Usually, I don't make New Year's resolutions. I believe if
something is worth doing it shouldn't require (or wait for)
a New Year's resolution; but in this year, I wanted to
make clear to myself that leisure time was important. I
had no worries about working hard and enjoying my job. I
seemed to have no trouble finding ways to do that. What I
needed was the self-discipline to enjoy leisure time, such as
reading.

I was successful. I managed to read fifty-two novels that year, though I had to select several short ones in December to make it to fifty-two! The change in life style became a habit. After several months of finding time to read, I found myself always carrying a novel. Anytime I find myself in a line (at the bank, post office, supermarket, etc.), I happily pass the time reading. One summer day with the family at Disneyland in Anaheim, I read all of *Ethan Frome* by Edith Wharton while waiting in lines (for the more popular attractions) that others found interminable. Several people during the day commented that they had wished they had thought of bringing a book. For many years beginning with 1985, I have averaged more than one novel per week without any new resolutions or effort. My reading has brought me profound enjoyment. And as with music, enjoying the outdoors, and many other pastimes, there is an essentially unlimited (and cheap) supply of the desired commodity. Reading novels is obviously not for everyone. But we each have some accessible activity we would like to engage in more often. Well, sit down and rearrange your life to accomplish this!

The phrase "I wish I had more time for..." is heard all too often. It may not be difficult to convert that wish to reality. Just as it is critical to learn to say "no" to some inessential and unrewarding activities, it's vital to learn how to say "yes" to pleasurable ones. Rearranging your life in this fashion involves better management of your time but it also involves discipline—the discipline to enjoy life. I will devote an entire chapter to the topic of self-control later in this book; but sometimes there is something more basic needed: articulate your goals.

This may seem trivial to most of us. Of course, we know what we would like to be doing now and what we would like to be doing in five years' time. The problem is the substantial one of coming up with a plan to ensure that we are doing what we'd like to be doing now and what is necessary to achieve our goals for the future. Many of us haven't gotten that far. We're not sure what we'd like to be doing tomorrow, much less five years from now.

Sometimes, deciding what one wants to do with one's life really requires only some reflection. Some individuals don't like to come to grips with hard choices, preferring to drift along, never looking beyond their next vacation or sometimes, their next coffee break! An unfortunate consequence of such aimless drifting is that years may pass unproductively. Time may be spent on activities, occupational or leisure, that would never have been selected if the individual spent some time confronting his or her desires and the various options for fulfilling them. The self-control techniques we will be discussing later are powerful tools for restructuring your life so that you maximize your chances of fulfilling your goals. You have to provide the goals.

Consider your present situation. If you are content with the broad canvas of your life, then you need only consider ways in which details may be added or altered to make life even more enjoyable and more meaningful or productive. But if you are not content, you need to ask yourself what would make you content. When you come up with a realistic set of goals, you can then set about trying to decide how to implement them; that is, how to get from your present situation to the desired one as efficiently and enjoyably as possible. As you begin to move toward your objectives, you will develop a sense of accomplishment and confidence, even excitement that in itself should make you a happier individual.

Now it's time to resume my story. We return to this issue of accomplishing one's goals, by discussing the behavioral principles underlying self-control (and the lack of it in many situations) as well as techniques that put these principles to work for us. Before we continue, there is one more principle I'd like to illustrate here. Recall that I felt elated when I thought (erroneously as it turned out) that my cancer had not spread beyond the prostate gland (based on the negative test results I received one week after my diagnosis of cancer). Others wondered why I was in such good spirits. "Have a good weekend, if you can," one friend said, implying that given my week-old diagnosis of cancer, I should be in poor spirits. Learning that there was no evidence of metastasis (spread) gave me a big boost psychologically, corresponding to the statistical boost in my life expectancy. My outlook may have been questionable compared to what it had been before the positive cancer diagnosis but it was dramatically improved over the uncertainty of the intervening week before the negative metastasis result.

This principle (known as delay-reduction) can work to our benefit. Given the grim news I was later to receive, or, more generally, given the tragic circumstances that sometimes confront us, it is important to move forward and not dwell on the gloomy aspects of our situation, nor the apparent better luck of others, nor on what might have been. Instead, activities which create even a small improvement in the present undesirable situation will be rewarding or highly valued and will support similarly constructive activities. These activities, if they produce outcomes which reduce the delay to a goal (hence "delay-reduction"),[1] will improve our situation, subjectively and objectively.

I found myself being pulled out of my shock and gloom as I took small steps to improve my situation. If I had just two or three years left, I could not afford to spend them in any way less than optimal; so, I directed most of my energy to an enjoyable immediate future. The very act of doing so made a positive difference.

Let's return now to those post-Halloween days as we struggled to deal constructively with a situation that we had to make, first tolerable and then enjoyable.

---

1. Numerous studies of choice behavior, i.e., studies in which subjects choose between different outcomes, have supported the following conclusions: We decide not on the absolute merit of the outcome, but on how much improvement in merit each outcome has compared to the situation in effect at the time of choice. To take a crude example, $10 is a much bigger reward to a pauper than $1000 to a multi-millionaire since the $10 brings about a relatively greater improvement to the pauper than the $1000 to the rich individual.

tips for living ─────────────────────

REPLACE SELF-DEFEATING STATEMENTS (your private thoughts and verbal statements) with positive statements. Tell yourself that you can move beyond the labels of the illness or event that has triggered stressful reactions in you. You are more than a label, such as *cancer victim.* You may find that *survivor* is a good word to help you handle your circumstances. Acting like a survivor, not a victim, affects how others (friends, family, and physicians) treat you and this, in turn, affects how you feel about yourself. Strive to feel and project positive emotions, because a positive outlook is contagious. This is more than just thinking positive thoughts; again, this is about doing things and saying things that show others how you feel about yourself.

SET GOALS TO LIVE. Whether a wedding, a child's graduation, a special trip you've always wanted to take, set the goal to be there.

FOCUS ON WHAT YOU CAN DO to improve your situation and what you can do to fully enjoy life. Whenever possible, minimize or eliminate your least rewarding activities. Often this simply means saying a polite, "No."

MAINTAINING A SENSE OF CONTROL reduces stress and strengthens your immune system. Even controlling small areas during aversive events helps, so set up every opportunity to have some freedom of choice when dealing with bad situations.

MAKE REASONABLE COMPROMISES between the extremes of always living for the moment and preparing for a secure future. Involve your family, for example, in decisions such as what to do about an anticipated home purchase or in selling your current home and moving to the lake or in sizing down to a more livable setting, and so on. Remember that others are living with you and for you and their needs matter too.

You must address their fears and concerns as you move forward.

LET YOUR CHILDREN IN on what is happening at a level and detail appropriate to their age. Involve them in your journey and express your love for them with words and deeds. Make them a part of your team, rather than treating them as outside observers.

SET ASIDE SPECIFIC WAYS TO REWARD YOURSELF! Exercise, read, and spend time with family. Always remember that "when I have time" often never happens unless you make the time. Ironically, you must have discipline to schedule personal leisure.

AVOID AIMLESS LIFE DRIFT by articulating your goals and the specific plans for achieving them. These articulations can be for the week or day, not always for larger amounts of time, not always about big accomplishments.

DO NOT DWELL ON THE GLOOMY ASPECTS of your situation, the better fortunes of others, or what might have been. Engage in activities that create even small improvements in any current undesirable situation.

life begins at eighty

There was a popular radio show when I was young called "Life Begins at Eighty." This was back in the early 1950s before television was king. In fact, this was still in the days portrayed by Woody Allen's memorable 1987 movie, "Radio Days." The movie, about a young boy growing up in Queens, New York, faithfully portrayed the central place radio had in the American family's heart and hearth. I, too, grew up in Queens and one of our favorite entertainments would be to take a subway into Manhattan ("The City," as we called it then) and be part of a live audience for popular radio shows such as "Your Hit Parade" and "Twenty Questions." These were free enter- tainments if you could get the tickets. On two or three occasions, I attended "Life Begins at Eighty." As I recall, the theme of the show focused on the plans of octogenari- ans (different each week) and the point was that a rich life lay ahead with some thoughtful planning. I don't know what the life expectancy of the average eighty-year-old is, but probably most octogenarians have a sense that their years are numbered. But these years may be wonderful ones, especially if they include goals and the plans for achieving them.

I, too, had to make certain that my numbered years were well spent. Like the octogenarian, I had to live as I could to help that number be as large as possible. I've already discussed how I rearranged my life to try to fulfill my most important goals, for what I hoped would be at least a five-year period. In this chapter, I'll discuss the treatment decisions we made and the role played in the treatment by alternative options, such as a macrobiotic diet and Kundalini Yoga; but first, a few words about my attitude, since we've made the point that a positive attitude is potentially a vital ally in the fight against stress and in the service of a heartier immune system.

Once I became used to the idea that I would be lucky to have five more years to live (remember, the five-year survival rate in my case was 29 percent), I was able to focus on the many everyday wonders life has to offer: not just an enhanced appreciation of the scenic and floral world around us, not only the cultural riches that I had yet to tap, not just my daughters' smiles, but also my professional activities pruned down as they were to a more manageable, enjoyable package, and my social interactions. I won't try to convey my heightened sensitivity to the beauties of the oceans, deserts, and mountains I looked at more clearly than before. I am not a poet. Nor am I a literary critic or musicologist who could bring alive for you the magic of a passage in Dickens or the adagio movement of Mozart's Third Violin Concerto. But, something interesting and exciting happened in my reactions to events that I can convey.

Before my illness, I was more sensitive and more affected by negative events in my life than by positive ones. Thus, having one of my research papers rejected by a journal caused me more grief than an acceptance would cause me joy. Perhaps I had been spoiled by success, but the rejection seemed more noteworthy and depressed me for a while. Not any more! When something positive happens, such as acceptance of a paper, I savor the success. Why should a rejection trouble me? Compared to my health prognosis, why should I be troubled by a rejected paper? Another example involves sports. Like most Americans, I am a sports fan. How did my illness affect my appreciation of sports? If my teams did well, I savored the victories and read about them in the sports pages; but if they did poorly, what did I care? This was truly only a game and I had better things to be emotionally involved with than a bunch of highly paid athletes. Again, I was able to enjoy the good aspects while ignoring the bad. One is reminded of the phrase, "having your cake and eating it too." Or perhaps the notion of "a free lunch" is more apt. Here was one case where I could take the good without the bad. In other words, thanks to my illness I put into action a credo many of us adhere to in principle but find very difficult to live up to in practice: accentuate the positive.

We all know the story of the half-filled cup. Do we emphasize that it is half full or that it is half empty? Since my illness I had become very much of a half full person, appreciating, even treasuring what I have. And this kind of attitude, provided that it does not lead to ignoring problems that must be dealt with, is almost a guarantee of contentment. So, paradoxically, it took a confrontation with my mortality to make me appreciate the joy of living to a degree I had never experienced before; and perhaps I had five more glorious years to look forward to!

As I mentioned earlier, Stephanie started us on a macrobiotic diet on Friday, November 4, just four days after my operation. I was well enough to accompany her to one of the local health food stores to acquire provisions.

Meanwhile she had arranged an appointment for us to meet with a macrobiotic counselor in San Diego. This appointment was sandwiched between appointments with three medical doctors (our Scripps urologist, a UCSD urologist for another opinion, and a Scripps radiologist). Each appointment was rather unique; each was an excellent source of information, albeit conflicting information, and each provided us with options to consider and pros and cons to weigh. The meeting with the macrobiotic counselor was the most unique. He was the only one of the four who suggested the realistic possibility of a cure for my condition. And even though intellectually I know that logic and statistics were on the side of the doctors and that my cancer was at an incurable stage, I admit it was refreshing to hear an optimistic opinion.

We arrived at the macrobiotic center where, as is customary in both macrobiotic and yoga centers, we removed our shoes before entering (an Asian influence). The fairly barren room contained sayings by Michio Kushi who is one of the leading exponents and authors of the macrobiotic movement. Also one sign made it clear that, by law, advice concerning medical conditions was not to be provided here. After a short wait the counselor arrived for what proved to be a two-hour consultation (for which he charged $75, by the way). The two hours involved a review of my past health habits, particularly dietary, my present habits and medical condition, a discussion of the theory and practice of macrobiotics, some predictions about what might occur should I persist on a strict macrobiotic diet, and quite a lot of advice.

As I was to learn, macrobiotics stresses the link between dietary history and current medical problems. I had been a large consumer of meat and dairy products (and alcohol, particularly wine and beer) before easing into vegetarianism in the 1970s. Thus, a macrobiotic counselor would point to these dietary habits as at least facilitators for my prostate cancer. The theory of macrobiotics can be related to on at least two levels. One was the language of macro-biotics in terms of countervailing forces of yin and yang. From the onset I found this language difficult to compre-hend. The theory which this language articulated was dif-ficult for me, a scientist, to appreciate; but I listened patiently, for I was not going to hear the practical sugges-tions without the theory that motivated them. I came to realize, however, that there was a second level of theory that I could relate to. Over the coming months I learned that many of the cornerstones of the macrobiotic diet had corresponding justifications in the nutrition literature. I'll share two incidents with you.

A close friend of ours is a linguistics professor at UCSD. Back in 1988 we were running partners. Naturally, in my period of decision (and indecision!) we often discussed my medical condition and options during our runs in Torrey Pines Park. When I told him about our macrobiotic diet, he surprised me by relating that he had been on such a diet for about eight years, while living in the Boston area. His reason for going on the diet involved a health prob-lem. His reason for giving it up was the inconvenience of staying on the diet, especially the restrictions it imposed on eating out with friends. During those eight years, dra-matic changes occurred in his health and he spent time in libraries trying to understand macrobiotic theory, rather than ignoring it, as has been my approach. He studied nutrition and human physiology and concluded that much of what constitutes macrobiotics is maximally suited for optimal digestion, nutrition, and well-being. These aspects include a wide range of those characterizing the macrobi-otic diet, from nutritional balance at a general level to the order of food eaten within the meal at a more specific level. Although macrobiotic theory is not expressed in the language of physiology, its practices are consistent with what is known, and becoming known, about good nutrition.

What of our friend's health before, during, and after his years on a macrobiotic diet? He states that those years were the best of his life in terms of feeling fit. Before and since that time he has been perpetually annoyed by sniffles and frequent colds. During those eight years he had neither. So he strongly endorsed my trying the diet based on his experience and on his library research. At the same time, he expressed serious skepticism about the possibility that any diet could actually reverse the progression of cancer.

The second incident occurred after I began radiation treatment in January of 1989 (about nine weeks after my operation). The radiologist knew that I was on a macrobiotic diet. He said that in order to reduce the discomfort and side effects of the radiation therapy (which involved daily radiation for, as I recall, thirty-seven treatments), I should be on a special diet. Since he knew I was committed to my own diet, however, he would not insist on my following his special diet. In fact, he was satisfied not even to go over it with me as long as I was aware that I could ask his assistant about it should my discomfort move me to do so. A couple of weeks later his assistant asked me just what a macrobiotic diet entailed. As I described it, she looked surprised. When I was finished she said, "Well those are precisely the diet measures we recommend for our radiation patients. You *are* on our special diet."

Let us return to that November meeting with the macrobiotic counselor. He professed strong optimism that I would be alright. He urged against risking intestinal damage with radiation and said that the macrobiotic diet was all that I would need to recover. He made some predictions. If I went on a strict macrobiotic diet I should experience what is known as discharge as, under the influence of the diet, my body disgorges a lifetime's accumulation of toxins, including those related to my cancer. He also predicted that the blood test monitoring my cancer (in my case the PSA test) would improve without medical treatment and that if it did so, perhaps I would have the good sense to avoid such treatment. We'll soon see how these predictions fared.

As for the diet itself, we were presented with a long list of foods to eat and foods to avoid. Some foods could be eaten with every meal, others only two or three times a week, others only very occasionally, and others not at all. The foods to be avoided included all meats, dairy products, most herbs, spices, supplements, and stimulants. For the first two weeks no oil was to be used in cooking or otherwise. Instead, the emphasis is on whole grains, primarily brown rice which should constitute about 50 percent of one's diet, and well-cooked vegetables. In addition, I was to have miso soup once a day (a soup flavored with Japanese soybean paste which lovers of Japanese cuisine are familiar with), small servings of sea vegetables (of which there are a surprising number of delicious varieties in addition to nori, the familiar black sheets used to wrap sushi), and I was permitted to drink various teas, primarily a Japanese tea known as "bancha" or "kukicha" made from the twigs, not the leaves, of the plant (and, therefore low in caffeine and tannin).

The diet is a dramatic departure from the Standard American Diet (or SAD). Yet, except for the seaweed (and the optional tea, which actually tastes very much like everyday gourmet tea), the ingredients are very basic, common foods. Once labeled *macrobiotic,* the foods took on a different aspect in some individuals' eyes. I recall eating lunch in my office one day with a container of rice and steamed vegetables (carrots, broccoli, and kale) when a colleague came visiting. He looked at my food container with thinly disguised disgust and exclaimed, "So that's what it looks like!"

By the way, despite eating prodigious amounts, I lost weight on the diet. My appetite is voracious and the food delicious, a combination designed to put on pounds. But the food, largely fat-free, is so low in calories and high in roughage that I lost twenty pounds in the first two years on the diet! Since I had been slender to begin with, I took on a gaunt, skin-and-bones appearance that led friends to conclude quite naturally that my weight loss was a result of the ravages of cancer. Anyone who saw the enthusiasm with which I ate, however, could not help suspect that I must not be so ill. In fact, I had been told that I should eat less in an effort to slow down my metabolism—and perhaps the rate of cancer growth as well. In any event, my counselor asked me to lose weight and assured me that weight loss was an almost inevitable consequence of a macrobiotic diet. He also predicted that, after a time, my weight would become stable, perhaps after regaining some of the lost weight. In fact, after two years I gained back five pounds while on our trip to New Zealand and Australia in 1991 (yes, we made it up the Stuart Highway, through the Red Center of Australia seeing Ayers Rock, the Olgas, Katherine Gorge, and Kakadu, among many other fabulous places, and thereby fulfilling one of our ambitions). In the years since, my weight has remained amazingly stable and about ten pounds below my weight in October 1988.

We had also read that the diet reduces sex drive for the first year or so. I, too, experienced a somewhat diminished sex drive, for two years. And it recovered somewhat at the same time my weight did, in 1991, while in Australia. We'll see later that this suggestive covariation also coincided with variation in my PSA blood test, leading us to an interesting speculation about one possible mechanism whereby the diet might be helping to resist my cancer.

How difficult was the transition to the diet for me? While I had been a heavy consumer of dairy products, I had long been a lover of vegetables and grains so the transition to a macrobiotic diet turned out to be easy in my case. Moreover, Stephanie, an excellent chef, was willing to devote time to some marvelous recipes that provided our diets with considerable variety. In fact, judging from my observations of other people's diets, our diet is considerably more varied than most; but that is not how other people see it. "Don't you get tired eating the same thing every meal?" is a question I have been asked many times. There are scores of available vegetables, especially in California, and they may be cooked in various ways and in various combinations. So, too, numerous whole grains are available which also may be prepared in various ways and combinations such as various types of rice, rye, barley, millet, whole wheat pasta, buckwheat pasta (or the Japanese soba), couscous, bulgar wheat, buckwheat, amaranth, quinoa, whole wheat berries, oats and corn (as in the Italian polenta). A legitimate question might be, "Don't you get tired of eating so much rice?" Even though almost half my diet consists of brown rice, after almost twenty years on the diet, I can honestly answer "no." In fact, I appreciate rice more now than I did prior to the diet, when I had preferred pasta and bread. One reason is that we generally pressure cook the rice and pressure-cooked brown rice is incredibly good to our taste.

For protein, a variety of beans are acceptable, especially the marvelous adzuki beans, as are soybean products such as tempeh (my favorite; often used in Indonesian cooking), tofu, seitan (made from wheat gluten; this tastes somewhat like meat which is probably why I am not too partial to it), and light fish (but not more than every ten days or so).

The reader who is interested in a macrobiotic diet (and I only wish I had discovered it sooner) may want to consult any one of a number of excellent introductions (such as *The Macrobiotic Way* by Michio Kushi, *Cooking the Whole Foods Way* by Christina Pirello, or *Cooking for Regeneration* by Cecile Levin). The diet may not be for everyone and there is no proof that it has helped me. I'm fortunate in that I find the food incomparably good. Later we'll see how I responded to the diet and I'll relate one rather convincing testimonial; but, first, we return to my days of gathering information and to a brief description of our visits to two distinguished urologists.

Our first visit was to a UCSD urologist, renowned for his research on prostate cancer. He looked over my file, including slides of the lymphatic involvement, and then gave me a thorough examination. His diagnosis was the same but his advice was different than I had received from my distinguished Scripps urologist. He favored a very aggressive treatment. Unlike my Scripps urologist, who recommended no action until symptoms developed, the UCSD urologist advocated aggressive treatment immediately, including two hormone-controlling drugs and radiation to the local prostate area. One drug was already FDA approved but at that time required daily self-administration by injection (lupron); the second (flu-tamide) was not yet FDA approved and would require pro-curement from nearby Mexico where it was available over the counter. Together these two drugs should block release of male hormones (testosterone), on which the hormone-dependent prostate cancer cells thrive. The radiation of the prostate area would, hopefully, eliminate cancer in the prostate gland itself, and perhaps, as a consequence, reduce the spread of the cancer elsewhere. Despite his advocacy of aggressive treatment, the UCSD urologist cautioned against radiation beyond the prostate. This could only produce debilitating side effects. From his examination this urologist felt that spread throughout the lymph system was already extensive and therefore, radiation of the lymph system in the pelvic area was pointless. In fact, his physical examination suggested that the lymph nodes in my neck area were already affected. In general, he portrayed a picture of a fairly advanced, fairly aggressive cancer. We were depressed that afternoon! At the same time, he suggested that aggressive treatment might significantly enhance my survival duration. We asked if there was anything we should do, in terms of diet, and he said, "No, just avoid red meat, but just from looking at you I can tell you are doing that already."

We gave this advice for an aggressive treatment prolonged consideration as we walked along the beach in Del Mar; a beach, that, this evening, seemed a bit grayer and less inspiring than the beach we loved. The prognosis seemed grim and the by-products of aggressive treatment seemed unfortunate (the impotence component, alone, would have been devastating news a few weeks earlier). We kept returning to the same conclusion: Aggressive, state-of-the-art medical treatment offered the best hope for being among the lucky 29 percent who survive five years.

So, we tentatively decided to keep on with our macrobiotic diet and to pursue aggressive treatment. I phoned a friend and former student who taught at a branch of San Diego State University at Calexico, on the border with Mexico, who readily agreed to procure the flutamide for me when I was ready to begin. It remained to discuss this approach with my Scripps urologist.

Our urologist made it clear that he disagreed with his colleague's recommendation. He said if I was enjoying life, why not continue to do so without the debilitating effects of the drugs and radiation, until I developed symptoms that were themselves debilitating? We went over the arguments that had been presented to us in favor of the aggressive approach. The doctor paused and said, "I'll be right back." He returned with the latest copy of *The Urology Times* and asked us to read a front-page story, written by a former student of the UCSD urologist. It was not the kind of story a doctor generally gives his patients. Normally doctors tend not to dwell on the negative aspects of a situation, especially an incurable one, and our urologist's emphasis was certainly on maintaining a positive attitude and trying to beat the statistics. The article addressed preliminary studies evaluating the very type of aggressive treatment that we were proposing (or at least its centerpiece, the two antihormone drugs). Its conclusion was that we had not progressed beyond orchiectomy (castration) in terms of improving the survival duration of metastasized prostate cancer patients. In other words, this recent article in a specialty medical journal suggested that the aggressive treatment that had been suggested for us was not a breakthrough.

We appeared to be at a standstill. Our doctor paused and said that he had a patient who was in a similar situation but who, unlike us, was trying to avoid aggressive treatment. This patient had instead gone on a macrobiotic diet in order to improve his immune system, and his PSA had come way down, close to normal. After mentioning this there was a long silence. The doctor was letting his words sink in and, presumably, was not going to take the extra step of recommending a macrobiotic diet for me. Meanwhile I was close to falling out of my chair. Up to now I had been carefully concealing our adoption of a macrobiotic diet from doctors since I thought they would think this an eccentric or soft-minded step and would be less likely to treat us as intelligent individuals, capable of evaluating scientific information. (Indeed, when our radiologist phoned me a few weeks later to ask what we had decided about radiation therapy, we explained that we were first assessing the effects of our macrobiotic diet. He thanked us for being so forthcoming, and said that most people wouldn't admit that. So we realized that our reluctance to talk to doctors about our exploration of untraditional approaches was perhaps typical.)

I broke the silence by noting that we had already begun a macrobiotic diet. Our doctor then made the same suggestion our macrobiotic counselor had made: stay on the diet for a few weeks and see if the PSA test improved before opting for aggressive treatment. We agreed, with a good measure of relief. Although intellectually we had decided on and were resigned to aggressive treatment, we were not looking forward to the daily radiation sessions, the taking of two fairly new drugs, and to the changes in life style, that all of this would bring. It was now mid-November and we were looking forward to the holiday season, and to our daughter Marin's fifth birthday on Thanksgiving day. A decision which we could justify to ourselves that entailed delaying aggressive treatment past the New Year was a welcome one, even if we expected that it was only a postponement, not a cancellation, of such treatment. In any event, we left Scripps Clinic that Friday afternoon feeling somewhat buoyant: we were delaying biting the bullet of aggressive treatment and we felt an additional glimmer of hope from our macrobiotic diet strategy.

A few weeks later, the next part of our strategy unfolded. Stephanie had suggested I take up yoga to help reduce stress in the upcoming months, especially given what I would likely have to live through, both physically and emotionally. While I did some new breathing exercises and learned to breathe through my nose instead of my mouth (a surprisingly easy change to make), I had neither the time nor inclination to become very serious about yoga. However, some time in early or mid-December, I received an article in the mail from an acquaintance who was a researcher at the nearby Salk Institute and who happened also to be a teacher of Kundalini Yoga. His research stressed ultradian rhythms especially involving the nasal cycle. I knew David from encounters in our local supermarket and we had exchanged scientific reprints in the prior year or so. The article he sent me was a preprint (that is a photocopied version of a manuscript that had not yet been published) that was to appear in a Handbook on Stress with chapters by several different neuroscientists. I assumed David sent it to me as a con-tinuation of our prior reprint exchange. In fact, I learned later, David had heard of my medical condition through mutual friends at Salk. He hoped I would read the article and, on my own, see its potential relevance for my condition. As it developed I did.

The article was an interesting review of the area in which David works. What distinguished it from most arti-cles appearing in scientific texts and journals was a section of applications at the end—applications of Kundalini Yoga to reduce stress. One of the techniques particularly caught my eye. It was a technique used for many years to combat cancerous tumors. It involved some breathing instructions that culminated in three deep breaths and exhalations. After the third exhalation one did not breathe again for at least one and up to three minutes. The rationale of the exercise is as follows: The lack of oxygen triggers an emergency reaction that in turn activates the body's immune system. The article said this exercise could be performed up to three times a day.

I tried it. Why not? I had nothing to lose and it was hard to see any negative side effects to this exercise. Nor was it time consuming. At first, it was all I could do to exhale and not breathe again for a minute or two. Soon, however, I could reliably exceed two minutes and sometimes reached three. I felt quite relaxed afterwards. I felt that it was good stress control even if it didn't deliver the big payoff it promised.

Was I doing it correctly? We phoned David and made an appointment to see him the day after Christmas. We went over that technique, learned that I had been doing it correctly, and David spent three hours going over a variety of other Kundalini Yoga techniques that were designed to strengthen the immune system and/or to eliminate toxins. He suggested I pick and choose among them. As it developed, I embraced almost all of them. Unfortunately, when added together they take time, up to three hours per day. However, I decided on the advice of David and my macrobiotic counselor (also a David) to give up potentially stressful physical activities such as long-distance running and bicycling and replace them with walking and yoga so that the extra investment in time was not so extreme. (I had commuted to UCSD, a six-and-one-half-mile ride that involves a steep 1.7-mile hill.)

For those interested in techniques of Kundalini Yoga for stress management and self-regulation, I can recommend two sources. First, there is the very chapter that helped me so much, by David Shannahoff-Khalsa (1991). Second, there is Yoga Bhajan's *Survival Kit: Meditations and Exercises for Stress and Pressure of the Times* (1980), an excellent and broad survey.[2] David's chapter describes techniques for alleviating emotional anxiety and stress, for lessening fatigue and listlessness, for expanding and integrating the mind, for regenerating the central nervous system, and for stimulating the immune system. In addition, David includes a technique for alleviating obsessive-compulsive disorders which ongoing research suggests is remarkably effective in controlled clinical settings.

To give you the flavor of the suggested techniques, I include here one on easing emotional stress and anxiety:

> "Sit and maintain a straight spine. Relax the arms and the hands in the lap. Focus the eyes on the tip of the nose (the end you cannot see). Open the mouth as wide as possible, slightly stressing the temporal-mandibular joint, and touch the end of the tongue tip to the upper palate where it is hard and

---

2. The complete reference to D. Shannahoff-Khalsa's chapter is Shannahoff-Khalsa, D. (1991). *Stress Technology Medicine: A New Paradigm for Stress and Considerations for Self-Regulation.* In *Stress: Neurobiology and Neuroendocrinology,* M.R. Brown, G. Koob, and C. Rivier (Eds.), New York: Marcel Dekker. See also: Shannahoff-Khalsa DS, *Kundalini Yoga Meditation: Techniques Specific for Psychiatric Disorders, Couples Therapy, and Personal Growth,* W. W. Norton & Company, New York, London, 2006.

The book can also be reviewed on the W. W. Norton web site at: www.wwnorton.com/NPB/nppsych/070475.html

Copies of Yogi Bhajan's manual can be obtained at www.a-healing.com

smooth. Breathe through the nose only, while making the breath long, slow, and deep. Let the mental focus be on the sound of the breath, listen to the sound of the inhalation and exhalation. Maintain this for at least 3-5 minutes with a maximum of 8 minutes at first trial. With practice, it can be built up to a 31 minute maximum." (Shannahoff-Khalsa, 1991, page 674)

Beginning on Tuesday, December 27, I launched a comprehensive Kundalini Yoga program that I have continued daily to this very morning, with some modification over the years. So now the two pieces were in place: a macrobiotic diet and Kundalini Yoga. How did I react to these central innovations in my life style and did they impress the detached recorder of the PSA blood test?

The answer to the second question is simple and unfortunately negative. In January, my PSA retest had not improved, but there were some interesting visible changes in my body and some dramatic changes in my feelings of well-being that led me not to lose heart. Before coming to the next major decision point after learning of the PSA result, I should discuss these changes.

Recall that David, our macrobiotic counselor, had predicted that I would observe discharges from my body as it eliminated toxins under the influence of the diet. Stephanie learned of such discharge in the macrobiotic literature she consulted. The discharges were said to consist of a variety of symptoms, including the one that I developed: swelling in the arms and legs. On two or three occasions I developed such extensive swelling that I had difficulty walking. This reaction continued for several weeks. David was surprised that the swelling continued for such a long period of time and predicted that there would be no blood test improvement until after the visible discharge was complete. What was going on? To this day, I don't know. One possibility is that the reaction was in part or wholly a food allergy to some component of the diet and had nothing to do with discharge. If so, the allergy cleared up on its own, because after a month, the symptoms terminated as abruptly as they had come, and have never troubled me since. One observation about the discharge intrigues me. Neither Stephanie, who went on the diet with the same completeness and enthusiasm as I did, nor our linguistic friend, who had been on the diet years before, encountered any discharge. It may, of course, be only coincidence; however, only I, the person whose body was in fact seriously compromised with disease, had the predicted discharge. Later, after I was to undergo radiation, I would periodically develop a rash at the site of the point of entry of the radiation (on my left hip). This rash would last several days, appearing monthly at first, then just occasionally, before ceasing altogether. I assumed that this was a normal reaction to radiation and was surprised when my radiologist said that he had not seen it before. He gave me a topical ointment which he said would get rid of it immediately, if it was not serious. It did. Having determined this, we agreed there was no need to use the ointment when the rash made its inevitable periodic appearance. According to macrobiotic theory, again the rash represents discharge (in this case from the radiation) induced by the macrobiotic diet. If so, one should not suppress it with medicine but should let it run its course. I'm not sure what we can conclude from these experiences of mine; however, I found the developments intriguing, if only suggestive.

What I can report with confidence is how I felt. The episodes of swelling in my arms and legs not withstanding, I found myself feeling more and more vigorous, especially after I added the yoga exercises to the diet. My appetite was voracious and my sense of well-being unparalleled. I had never felt this good before. Recall too that I was already in good physical shape (the minor matter of cancer always excepted) and had been running fifty miles per week, with a sub-three-hour marathon to my credit, and bicycling close to one hundred miles per week. So my sharp increase in subjective fitness was not simply the result of someone hopelessly out of shape feeling the benefit for the first time of a serious exercise regimen. The word *dynamic* best expresses my new sense of well-being. This feeling of exceptional well-being continued for at least a year or two, even through the daily insult of radiation. During this period I no longer was susceptible to colds (I had previously been a frequent cold sufferer) and when a flu bug passed through the family or my colleagues, I would either not get it at all or feel ill for just a few hours instead of days or weeks. Was it the diet and/or the yoga? Or was it sheer coincidence? I can't be sure, of course, but I personally doubt it was coincidence. I like to think that this change in my subjective fortunes was in turn a sign that the diet and yoga were having their intended effect of strengthening my immune system. If so, perhaps they would indeed be my allies in combating cancer.

I noted that the feeling of intense well-being and lessened susceptibility to disease lasted for a year or two. To this day it continues, only not to the same degree; I no longer feel I could chew nails, but I still feel extremely fit; I can no longer claim to be entirely free of ailments, but the few colds I've had in the past seventeen years have been extremely mild and short-lived. My only regret is not having pursued a macrobiotic diet and Kundalini Yoga all my life. As we have implied, regrets are not functional; I vigorously pursue both macrobiotics and yoga today and will continue to do so for my indefinite future.

When January came, so did time for the PSA test, the result of which I looked toward with great apprehension. Until now, I'd been harboring a dream, perhaps a fantasy, that I might be able to postpone further, even indefinitely, treatment. Perhaps diet and exercise alone would serve me well, at least for some time. When the phone call came with the test result, I was in the middle of a particularly strenuous yoga routine. Stephanie answered the phone and her tone quickly changed from one of anxiety to deep disappointment and frustration.

A month of our new regime, a month of quiet hope had produced no fruit. As Stephanie told me the news, I finished my strenuous exercise. It was clear from our disappointment that somewhere inside us, though we had never acknowledged it openly, we expected some improvement, some minor miracle that would have enabled us to avoid unpleasant alternatives. I suspect it was particularly hard for Stephanie who had invested such time in learning to prepare food the macrobiotic way. Cooking the kind of macrobiotic meal that Stephanie was preparing at least once a day (we had leftovers frequently) was labor intensive, especially when starting out; but, really, we were not in a different position than we had been a month earlier. We would continue the diet and exercise and we would now opt for aggressive treatment. An easier solution had not fallen in our laps, but perhaps the more difficult path would lead to one. I was reminded of my mother's request for a definitive resolution of my medical condition and my impish desire, barely checked, to reply, "The only quick resolution I can have is a quick death." There was to be no instant recovery.

We had to maintain a positive outlook, not only for ourselves, but also for our children and my aged parents who lived with us, in an attached apartment, and who proved to be experts at denial. My father referred to me as "cured" and my mother referred to prostate cancer as "so easy to cure." I sometimes had trouble curbing my frustration at their denial and optimism: "You'll see this is just a tempest in a teapot," my father mentioned one day when, of course, I should have been pleased that they were able to cloak themselves in a protective emotional shield.

When we saw our urologist again, he said he'd be willing to institute the complete aggressive treatment we were advocating, although he made it clear he still favored not tampering with my quality of life until such time as symptoms required treatment. He suggested a compromise; namely, begin local radiation of the prostate now but hold off on the hormonal therapy until the radiation was completed, and then only if my PSA was still elevated. He pointed out that it would be easier to tolerate the treatments in sequence and easier to evaluate their separate effects.

Probably we were in the same frame of mind as we had been in November: intellectually, we favored an aggressive approach, to be started immediately; emotionally, we welcomed the chance to postpone some or all of it, given arguments that we could use to rationalize our timidity. So again, we agreed to this compromise suggestion—an agreement we have never regretted.

Before undertaking the radiation, we were cautioned against it by both our counselors, macrobiotic and yoga. Each warned of the damage that the radiation might do and urged us to continue with their approach alone. In particular, the macrobiotic counselor was concerned about

potential damage to the intestines, a legitimate worry for
an approach that emphasizes the central importance of
good digestion. Once it became clear that we were going
ahead with the radiation, however, each counselor
suggested refinements of our regimens to minimize the
fallout from the treatment. In particular, the yoga instruc-
tor suggested an additional exercise designed to strengthen
the pelvic area while I was undergoing radiation. The macrobiotic counselor suggested three primary changes: miso
soup twice daily (instead of once); a large sheet of nori
(that seaweed used in sushi) each day; and fish once per
week. All these were believed to counter the side effects
of radiation, some of this belief based on Japanese
research following the atomic bombings at Hiroshima and
Nagasaki.

I won't describe the radiation procedures in detail. The
preliminary work involved a fair degree of discomfort, but
the thirty-seven radiation treatments themselves were
painless. Scripps Clinic is just a mile and one-half north
of UCSD and on my way home; so, I would leave work in
the late afternoon, walk briskly to Scripps for my daily
treatment and then hop a bus the rest of the way home.
The treatment itself took just a few minutes. There was
little waiting and what waiting did occur was in the presence of the same patients every day. I don't know what
their cancers were and how they are doing now, but I will
never forget their faces, their anxious looks, and their
good cheer. I hope they are doing well.

Occasionally I would overhear patients discuss side
effects with each other or with the sympathetic and
obviously competent nurses. Some of the effects were
rather ghastly and made me extremely grateful that I had
yet to encounter serious ones. As radiation progressed,
however, I did develop some reactions. The most serious

one was fairly intense rectal pain for several hours every morning, a pain that prevented me from concentrating. However, my radiologist said that I was sailing through the radiation, this pain notwithstanding. Within a day or two following completion of the radiation, I was pain-free once again. The serious side effects that might have developed (edema, impotence, and incontinence) never did; although I estimate that my rectum and bladder aged ten years.

Whether I was simply lucky in avoiding serious discomfort and potentially more serious side effects or whether the macrobiotic and yoga regimens and adjustments helped, I'll never know. In any event, it was a relief to have completed the treatments. Now we faced the question of if and when to institute the hormonal therapy. As each month went by, my PSA count was lower. There seemed good reason to postpone aggressive hormone therapy. Why was the PSA going down? Almost certainly the radiation had been at least partially responsible. As the PSA entered the normal range in the autumn of 1989, my radiologist, previously very skeptical (given my condition with demonstrated metastasis) that the PSA would fall to normal, became more optimistic, "We'll do it with just radiation," he enthused. My macrobiotic counselor seemed unsurprised. At our first meeting he had professed that the diet would be sufficient. He had said: "Of course the doctors see progression of the cancer as inevitable. They have seen thousands of cases, all following the same inexorable progression. But they haven't seen the effects of a macrobiotic diet. I have and I know it can alter that progression." Around the time the PSA entered the normal range, my yoga counselor saw me at the bus stop in Del Mar and gave me a lift to UCSD, near his laboratory at the Salk Institute. He asked what the doctors thought about my dramatic improvement. I replied that they were pleased, of course, but also seemed a bit puzzled. David beamed and said, "But we know better." I was pleased that everyone took credit for my improvement and, I continue to assume with profound gratitude, that all three aspects of my adjustments (radiation, macrobiotic diet, and Kundalini Yoga) played a role.

Of course, the fact that my blood test was now in the normal range in no way altered the fact that I had metastasized prostate cancer. Even by the most optimistic macrobiotic assessment, seven years must transpire before the cancer cells in my lymph system, and wherever else they had invaded, would be replaced. Remember, I had undergone no treatment for cancer that had spread beyond the prostate. Nonetheless, I was quite satisfied with my current status and felt more confident than ever that I would at least live to see the fulfillment of my five-year plan.

Perhaps, too, part of the credit for my improvement reflected the lessened stress I was experiencing as a result of my rearranged life style. Before I bring my personal story up to the present, I should discuss the principles of self-control. I am convinced that a knowledge of self-control is critical for the ability to structure one's life to maximize the likelihood of achieving one's central goals. In recent years a wealth of research studies have contributed to an appreciation of what determines whether we behave impulsively (opting for small short-term gain) or exercise self-control (opting for larger long-term gain). These studies have led to successful applications. In the next chapter, I discuss the more important basic research, in simple terms, and the strategies for self-control that this research has inspired.

tips for living ────────────────────

NO MATTER YOUR AGE, every year can be wonderful if you consistently set goals for living.

SAVOR EVERY SUCCESS and minimize negative events. Don't ignore problems, but follow this strategy and strive for contentment.

ATTEND TO THE MESSAGES your physical body is sending you and use those messages to determine the activities you should continue and those you should not.

REMEMBER THAT REGRETS CAN BE INSTRUCTIONAL, but are not functional. Move on with what you will do differently and then begin to do things that reduce the possibility of those things you regret. No better time than now exists to think about the small but important details of friendship, gratitude, and sharing with others how they have helped you learn or grow. Regrets are debilitating; thus, once you have acknowledged your pain, work to think about what a well-lived tomorrow will look like for you. Your past practices are not predestined to cloud your future.

EXAMINE THE DIFFERENCE BETWEEN OPTIMISM & DENIAL. The first inspires you to explore; the second blocks you from moving forward.

REARRANGE YOUR LIFE STYLE to promote self-control. Learn the techniques for rejecting impulsive behavior (choosing small, short-term gain) over self-control (opting for larger, long-term gain).

self-control

Self-control can generally be thought of as a choice between an immediate small reward and a delayed larger reward. For example, the small immediate reward might be a blueberry muffin for a dieting model, a cigarette for a chain smoker, or an extra hour of sleep for a lazy author. The larger delayed reward might be a trimmer figure, better health, or completion of a manuscript chapter. Selection of the immediate small reward is often considered impulsive while selection of the delayed larger reward is considered an instance of self-control.

Self-control was once thought to be a pattern of behavior found only in humans and perhaps some of the higher nonhuman primates. In recent years, however, we have learned that self-control may be demonstrated for lower animals as well. Moreover, it takes little reflection about the state of the world to realize that, in practice, self-control is demonstrated all too rarely by humans.

Indeed, many of society's problems stem from a preoccupation with short-term gain. This is most evident if we consider crime; however, the woeful dearth of self-control is manifest elsewhere. Consider the environment where the pressures for practical immediate solutions to industrial and political problems may lead to decisions that make good sense in terms of the next year (more housing or more jobs or lower taxes...the list goes on) but may wreak havoc with our environment in the longer term. We may foot the bill later in terms of poorer quality of life, higher rates of cancer, and a legacy of unsolved life-threatening problems for our grandchildren.

Industrial corporations are often plagued by an emphasis on short-term profits. Stock analysts and investors place tremendous emphasis on short-term earnings prospects as revealed in a company's quarterly reports. Often there is risk in undertaking long-term restructuring of the corporation or in taking measures that, while costly now, would produce a stronger corporation five years in the future. The specter of a mediocre, short-term outlook may trigger sell recommendations by analysts. The resultant selling of the company's shares erodes the investment of the shareholders. The corporate leaders who make the decisions are usually the largest shareholders, that is, the ones with the most to lose. So there is an inherent bias to favor short-term results, even though this bias may lead to relatively unfavorable long-term results, at least compared with the company's true potential, as results from a recent study have confirmed. Don't the leaders of corporations realize this? Don't they see that, ultimately, it is in the best interest of the corporation to adopt goals consistent with a longer-term perspective? Generally, yes, in the same way that a dieter knows that there is a greater long-term benefit in passing up an inviting muffin; in the same way that a smoker knows there is a greater long-term benefit in not lighting up; in the same way that I know there is a greater long-term benefit in getting out of bed when my alarm goes off to work on a research manuscript than there is in returning to sleep for an hour. The corporate leader faces the same pressures as the dieter, the smoker, and the sleepy professor: the pressure to accept the immediately available short-term gain. The corporate leader may not be part of the same corporation five years later so, in economic terms, the benefit of the long-term gain to the corporation may be discounted somewhat by the possibility that such gains may not benefit the individual.

Politicians face a host of comparable problems on a daily basis. Consider only the example of education. Money spent to better educate our youth should have several tangible and profound positive effects on our society. For example, with increased education our young will develop into adults who are fit for more skilled work positions which, in turn, will lead to reduction in crime and a more competitive economy. The catch is that these benefits are many years away and the costs are immediate. Also relatively immediate are the politician's re-election concerns, and he may perceive his re-election chances damaged by programs that cost the taxpayers money. Again, the bias is on making decisions that increase the likelihood of short-term gains at the expense of greater long-term benefits.

If in confronting major economic, educational, and environmental problems, society, with all of its resources, generally opts for small short-term gains rather than the greater long-term gains, what hope is there for individuals confronted with similar dilemmas? We shall see that individuals have some powerful behavioral strategies for self-control at their disposal that can be utilized to favor selection of the greater long-term goals!

Let us begin by reviewing some research that has helped us to understand the conditions under which individuals, and animals, either behave impulsively or demonstrate self-control. Remember, we say individuals behave impulsively when they choose the immediate (but smaller) short-term goal. We say individuals show self-control when they choose the delayed (but larger) longer-term goal.

The first experimental study of self-control with animals happens also to be the first research study I conducted as a first-year graduate student at Harvard in 1961-62. I was interested in seeing whether pigeons could delay gratification. Under what conditions would pigeons choose the larger, delayed reward (showing self-control) rather than the smaller, immediate reward (behaving impulsively)? In my study, hungry pigeons could obtain a food reward (grain) either by pecking a key immediately after it was illuminated with a red light or by delaying the peck until the light turned green. If the pigeon pecked at the red key, grain was made available immediately for three seconds, following which there was a penalty period in which no reward was available. This penalty was one minute in one condition of the experiment and was thirty minutes in another condition of the experiment. On the other hand, the pigeon could elect not to peck at the red key. In this case, following a delay time (of a few seconds; the time required varied across conditions), the light turned from red to green. By pecking at the green key light the pigeons could obtain grain without a subsequent penalty period. In addition, in some conditions the pigeons could obtain three three-second grain presentations by pecking at the green key light. In all conditions, after obtaining one or three rewards by pecking at the green key light, the green light reverted to red and a new choice trial was begun.

Did the pigeons wait for the green key light and, thereby, greatly increase their rate of reward? Or, did they behave impulsively and always opt for the immediate reward available by pecking the red key light, even though a penalty period, in which they could earn no reward, followed? Although my pigeons did not often exhibit self-control by delaying i.e., by waiting for the green light, their tendency to do so did increase in proportion to the advantages of delaying. In other words, the frequency with which the pigeons exhibited self-control by not pecking at the red key depended upon the relative attractiveness of conditions following pecks at the red and green keys.

Humans demonstrate self-control in a variety of sophisticated ways. Consider the classic example of Ulysses, who had himself tied to the mast of a ship to avoid being tempted by the Sirens. Ulysses determined at a distance that the avoidance of crashing upon the rocks outweighed the pleasure of approaching and better hearing the Sirens. Critically, Ulysses was shrewd enough to realize that the closer he got to temptation, the less likely that he would resist it. Thus he tied himself to the mast so that should his value-structure, his priorities, change, he would be committed to stick by his original decision not to be tempted. Many of us follow the same logic when we put an electric alarm clock out of easy reach so that we will not be able to turn it off without getting out of bed the following morning. This is done when the consequences of one behavior—getting up on time—are valued more highly than the consequences of another—sleeping late. In the morning, this preference may be reversed; but we are forced to rise from bed to turn off the alarm.

Ulysses, of course, is a mythological hero and even ordinary humans are complex organisms.

A study by renowed psychological researcher, Dr. George Ainslie shows that choice for a larger, delayed reward over a smaller, immediate reward becomes easier when the subject commits in advance to the larger reward. This advance commitment is necessary since the subject is much more likely to choose the smaller reward once it is immediately available. The advance commitment occurs because at the time the commitment is made the larger reward is preferred. As the rewards become temporally close, a reversal of preference occurs: immediacy of reward becomes more important than magnitude. Fantino and Navarick (1974) have considered such preference reversals in human self-control:

"For example, consider a reluctant dieter faced with the choice of a delectable hot-fudge sundae, a scoop of orange sherbet, or no dessert at all. His choice is based on taste and caloric content. If he is asked to order his dessert twenty-four hours before the meal to be served, he may well choose neither, since the caloric dimension may be more important to him at this time. As the meal approaches, however, taste becomes more important and preference may shift from omitting dessert to ordering sherbet.

When the sundae and sherbet are physically presented for choice at the actual meal, however, selection of the sundae becomes more likely, since the taste dimension should be most important at this time (as long as the eater is still hungry)" [Fantino and Navarick, 1974, pp.148-149].

Preference reversal with time also occurs commonly where unpleasant events are concerned. Often scheduling an appointment with a dentist is put off because of the negative reactions some individuals have toward the dental work. By scheduling the appointment far enough in advance, however, we are more likely to succeed: the positive benefit to our dental health will outweigh the negative reaction to impending discomfort. Thus we are more likely to schedule the appointment (commitment to the self-control choice) than not (impulsive selection). Another example involves the scheduling of medical check-ups for individuals fearful of negative news. Again, schedule the annual check-up far enough in advance when the self-control option looks more inviting.

If commitment occurs, as indicated by Ainslie's experimentation, because preference changes with time, then it should be possible to get preference reversal by having the subject choose at different times between two rewards. Indeed, Drs. Howard Rachlin and Leonard Green were able to demonstrate that preference for a small, immediate reward over a delayed, larger reward could be reversed by simply adding a constant amount of delay to both rewards.

The idea in their experiment, and in a later one I did with Dr. Douglas Navarick, is that when the delays are sufficiently long, selection of the larger reward is likely, just as selection of no dessert or sherbet is likely if the dieter is asked far enough in advance. But, when the delay to the actual choice is short, selection of the impulsive choice (for example, the sundae) becomes increasingly likely.

Rachlin and Green's interpretation of their results is a good illustration of the behaviorists' viewpoint. They note that self-control is a product of immediate environmental factors, whether we are referring to Buddhist monks, seven-year-old children, or pigeons. Generally, self-control appears to be a special case of choice behavior, controlled by the same laws that govern choice. The same factors that determine which of two options we select also determine whether we show self-control or behave impulsively.

Isn't it likely that we humans, with our complex brains and knowledge, could do a much better job of demonstrating self-control than we do typically? More generally, couldn't we arrange our environment to promote the longer-term gains we discussed earlier? There are at least four effective strategies for doing so.

First, there is the commitment strategy we have already encountered. Ideally we do what Ulysses did; that is, rearrange our environment to make the unwanted impulsive behavior essentially impossible. But, when that is difficult or undesirable, we can still promote commitment to the desired self-control option by building constraints on our behavior. A relatively weak, nonetheless helpful, form of commitment is simple public statement of your intention. If you tell your close friends that you will not eat dessert after dinner that night and request that they ask you if you abstained when seeing you the next day, the chances that you will indeed skip dessert are increased perceptibly. A technique that also enlists a friend's aid but has more teeth in it involves putting your money where your mouth is. In this case you write a substantial personal check to an organization that you loath (perhaps one that fills your mailbox weekly with junk mail requesting funds for a cause you detest; better yet, one that phones you at dinner time for the same despised cause). Give the check in a stamped envelope to a friend whom you can trust with the following instructions (assume here that you are giving up smoking): "If I smoke (for example if you see me smoking) then mail this check at once no matter what I say." Obviously the same approach can be used with weight loss (where the measure may be the weight registered on a scale) or any other behavior that is readily observed or measured. With weight loss, it is also important to replace unhealthy foods with more healthful ones.

A second strategy to enhance the likelihood of self-control is called *self-reinforcement*. Basically, this technique involves giving yourself a treat if and only if you accomplish some specified goal. For example, you can simply imagine something good happening when you pass up an impulsive option. Thus, the struggling dieter may imagine looking flabby in a bathing suit as the summer beach vacation approaches, while approaching the dessert area in a cafeteria; then, after successfully passing the desserts by, imagining a svelte figure in that same bathing suit. A more concrete (unimagined) reward is probably still more effective. For example, when I finish the page I am now writing, my third this morning, I will reward my accomplishment by stretching my legs and then spending ten minutes reading my current novel. The idea behind self-reinforcement is that the reward (or reinforcement) should strengthen the behavior it follows. Thus, reading my novel (a highly desired activity,) should strengthen the behavior it follows (writing this book), making it more likely that I will continue writing in the future (and if you are reading this I have at least been that successful!) There is a subtle but powerful point to be made here. Normally the two activities, writing this book and reading a novel, are competing activities; one may disrupt the other; but by arranging the relationship so that one follows the other, they become complementary, not competing, activities. One leads to the other so that the behaviors now go hand-in-hand instead of toe-to-toe.

Let us consider another example, making this point (though not one involving self-reinforcement) based on an actual experiment done by Dr. Lloyd Homme and his associates at the University of Kansas. The experiment involved three-year-old nursery school children. Behavior for these children was that typical of three-year-olds: talking, running around, and shouting. Paying attention to the teacher was not so prevalent. But Homme and his associates decided to see if the children's preferred behaviors could be used to strengthen the less-preferred behaviors of sitting in one's seat and paying attention to the teacher. The teacher announced to the children that if they remained in their seats and paid attention, after a period of time (a variable period) a bell would sound and the teacher would give an instruction such as "Run and Shout." At first, the bell sounded after just a few seconds of the children's attention and the students engaged in a short burst of running and shouting. Gradually the time between bell ringings was lengthened. By the second or third day, the teacher had achieved uncommon (even rapt) attention in the nursery school classroom, with less overall running and shouting than had taken place in the previously unstructured situation. By making running and shouting freely available after a period of sitting in seats and paying attention, the degree and duration of attention was increased by a remarkable degree. Running and shouting were now strengthening or complementing attentive behavior, instead of competing with it. Similarly, when we use self-reinforcement to increase the likelihood of engaging in the behaviors we desire to promote, we are often using potentially disruptive competing activities as rewards for strengthening the desired behavior.

Finally, there is another by-product or bonus that we gain when we employ self-reinforcement. When we give ourselves a treat for engaging in a desired (here, the self-control) activity or in passing up an undesired (impulsive) activity, we are making our achievement salient. That is, the self-reinforcement serves as a marker which forces us to note our success in this instance. As we shall see next, such record-keeping is itself a powerful self-control strategy.

I would argue that this third self-control strategy, record-keeping, should have a prominent place in any self-control program. This insight was forced upon me by the results of a little experiment I did with some undergraduate students many years ago. Three students in my learning and motivation course were anxious to assess some behavioral methods to help people quit cigarette smoking. (I don't now remember all of their names but I can at least give credit to one of them, who visited me some years later, and was by then, Dr. Fred Schindler). In particular, some filters were on the market that used what we call a fading procedure to eliminate the urge to smoke. These filters were to be attached to your cigarette. But each day's filter was slightly more opaque than the prior day's. After a month the filter was so thick that inhalation on the cigarette produced no nicotine. The idea of fading procedures, in general, is to introduce a change so gradually that it does not disrupt the behavior. In the case of the successively thicker filters, the idea is to reduce the nicotine content of the cigarettes so gradually that withdrawal reactions do not occur (for if they did occur, the smoker would be likely to abandon the filters altogether, thereby failing to quit). Fred and his two fellow students were more interested in testing the effectiveness of these filters in a controlled study.

We conducted a study, with a large group of UCSD students who responded to an advertisement in the school newspaper offering help to those who wanted to give up cigarette smoking. We then divided the volunteers into four groups, only three of whom I can recall clearly. One group used the filter approach. A second group employed a satiation technique in which subjects were required to smoke at a rapid rate (in synchrony with the experimenter's prompt to puff, every twenty seconds or so), inducing nausea. A third used some other promising technique and the fourth was our control group. As we noted earlier, a control group is typically included in studies of this type to assess any changes due to factors other than those specific to the treatments. One such factor, of course, is the mere passage of time. In order to be of import, any decline over weeks in smoking frequency seen in the treatment groups must be steeper than in the control group which receives no treatment. Remember that these subjects were volunteers who were seeking to give up smoking. So we need to know the extent to which their smoking frequency would have been diminished in the absence of treatment. Subjects in the control group have the expectation of being treated (and indeed were treated at the end of the study) which in itself might reduce smoking frequency.

How did we measure how much the subjects were smoking? We asked them to keep records of how many cigarettes they smoked each day. Since these were motivated volunteers, we felt we could rely on them to be reasonably accurate; and there was no reason to assume that any inaccuracies would favor one group rather than another. Ideally, a more rigorous method of record-keeping would have been desirable, but other solutions such as constant observation, were impractical.

We found that we were reasonably successful in eliminating smoking in our subjects. Most of them had stopped by the end of the study. What intrigued us most was that the control group, whose members simply kept a record of how much each smoked, without any treatment, did so well: Most of the control group subjects had also stopped smoking. There appeared to be little difference between the groups. What was going on?

We suspected the role of record-keeping, which was common to all groups, including the control group. So we next reviewed a large number of published studies which had included record-keeping control groups. Invariably, these groups did very well. We then realized that the mere act of record-keeping is an effective technique for changing the behavior in directions that we desire. Of course, an interesting question remains: why should record-keeping be such an effective self-control strategy?

There are at least two good reasons underlying the effectiveness of record-keeping as an instrument for behavioral change. In the first place it allows you—even forces you to observe and document your accomplishments and, therefore, helps you feel positive about them. Equally important, record-keeping doesn't allow you to fool yourself about your accomplishments. It keeps you honest. We have all known habitual dieters who are continually claiming that they hardly ate anything today, when we have seen them munching away regularly. Some would-be-dieters boast of not eating a single meal when in fact they have consumed a dozen small ones in the form of high-calorie snacks. Honest record-keeping doesn't allow the individual to get away with this type of self-deluding behavior. Once dieters are committed to writing down everything they eat (actual calorie-counting is best), they are confronted with the realities of their gastronomic excesses. Similar examples could be discussed from other areas. We all know children or students who claim they studied extensively when we have observed them wasting time prodigiously; we all know drinkers who claim and often believe they have had much less to drink than the facts would warrant.

I had a similar experience once. Leafing through a book

on life style and longevity in Del Mar's *Earth Song* book-
store, I came across a chart linking alcohol consumption
to longevity or rather the lack of it. The chart noted several different categories of drinking and assigned a risk
factor to each. I consumed a fair amount of wine with
dinner in those days but I didn't know my category (more
than forty drinks a week; twenty-four to thirty-nine
drinks; etc.). So I decided to keep track of how many
glasses of wine I had each day to find out what my category was. Immediately I noted several changes in my
behavior. First, I no longer casually topped my wine glass
off (or permitted my host to do so at a party) for this
would interfere with an accurate count. Second, when confronted at the end of dinner with a bottle of wine that
still contained enough for another glass or so I found that
I asked myself, "Do I really want another glass of wine?"
rather than treating the near-finished bottle as a cue for
impulsively pouring the rest into our glasses. Usually the
answer was no. More generally, the mere fact that I was
committed to noting each glass of wine I consumed made
me ask that question, "Do I really want one?" routinely.

It turned out that I never did establish how much wine
I had been drinking. As soon as I decided to keep track of
my wine consumption, I found myself drinking substantially
less, but savoring what I did drink all the more. Over several weeks of record-keeping, my wine consumption
declined, seemingly without effort.

Similarly, in a research project designed to enhance
study behavior (Fox, 1966), which we will discuss in more
detail later, students who recorded their daily productivity
continued at work on their assignments until they outdid

their preceding performances. Record-keeping contributed to continued improvement. In conclusion, the mere act of keeping a record of the frequency of a behavior you would like to control will be of dramatic assistance in helping you to control it.

The fourth behavioral strategy for self-control involves what we behavior analysts refer to as *stimulus control.* I have written extensively on this topic elsewhere.[3] The basic concept is straightforward. Assume that a response has been acquired in the presence of a particular stimulus or situation. If the same response is made when new stimuli are present (i.e., another situation) we say that stimulus generalization has occurred (the response has generalized to the new stimuli). If the same response is not made when these new stimuli are present, we say that discrimination has occurred: the new stimuli have been discriminated from the old ones.

For example, a child who has been bitten by a brown Afghan hound is likely to be more frightened by an Irish setter than by a fox terrier and is less likely to fear a horse or a Siamese cat than either type of dog. When the child reacts in the same (fearful) way to another animal as to the offending Afghan hound, we say his behavior is generalizing (imprecise stimulus control). When the child reacts in a non-fearful way to the other animal, we say that he is discriminating between the offending hound and the other animal (more precise stimulus control). It should be clear that many important phenomena involve

---

3. Chapter 5 in Fantino, E., and Logan, C.A. (1979). The Experimental Analysis of Behavior: A Biological Perspective. San Francisco, W.H. Freeman.

the processes of generalization and discrimination. Without generalization something learned in one situation could not be performed in even a slightly different situation. Without discrimination a behavior acquired in one situation would be displayed in all other situations, no matter how inappropriate. How we *categorize* sensory data, perceptions, and thoughts all involves generalization and discrimination and has ramifications for our beliefs and prejudices. But how may the principle of stimulus control be enlisted to promote self-control?

Behaviors are more likely to occur in situations where they occur habitually and where they have been enjoyed in the past. When the same or similar situations arise, reoccurrence of the behavior becomes likely. This may be viewed as an example of generalization. Similarly, old behaviors are less likely to reoccur in the presence of relatively novel situations (an example of discrimination). The extent to which the behavior will occur in a novel situation depends first on the similarity between the novel situation and those situations in which the behavior has occurred previously; and second, upon the past history of the behavior, whether it has been maintained in a wide variety of situations (imprecise stimulus control) or only in very specific circumstances (precise stimulus control). We can use these simple facts about stimulus control to rearrange our environment so that we manipulate the likelihood of behaving in ways that we desire. We'll consider two examples: one involving study behavior, the other dieting. We'll also consider a potential pitfall that can be usually foreseen and avoided.

The example involving the use of stimulus control to

promote study behavior comes from an experimental study by Ljungberg Fox [2005]. He had students set aside a place to study that was used only to study. In our case this might be a particular desk in our home or in a library. His instructions stressed that if the student felt the necessity to do something other than study (for example to daydream a bit or to talk with a friend), the student should leave the study area. In this way, all the stimulus cues in the study area would be associated with actual study and not with other competing activities. In this way, Fox found that his subjects came to study with greatly increased efficiency at their designated workplace. They also achieved progressively longer periods of concentrated study.

The same principle and strategy can be applied to dieting. Many of us are prone to eat almost anywhere in our home: kitchen, dining room, in front of the television, at our desk, and so on. Thus, the cues of eating are forever with us. If we want to eat less, an important step we can take is to gain more precise stimulus control over the cues that give rise to eating. Following the study behavior example, this means limiting these cues to one area. If we restrict eating to one area, the dining room, after a few days, thoughts of food in other areas of the house will begin to diminish. This technique has also been used successfully with insomniacs. They are instructed to use their bedrooms for sleep, but not for competing activities such as watching TV.

Once we have established relatively precise stimulus control over our actions, of course, then we can make further refinements. We can alter our exposure to the situations or stimuli, that exert control over the behavior we wish to adjust. For example, once a particular location has become particularly conducive for study, by spending more time in that location, study may be increased. On the other hand, once cues for eating are largely restricted to the dining room, we can avoid the dining room except at meal times.

Naturally, manipulating our environment to expose ourselves to the types of stimulus control that will promote behaviors we want to increase and avoid behaviors we want to decrease, is not always easy. Other techniques, such as the ones discussed earlier may be needed to help expose us to the appropriate cues. Thus, a student deciding on whether to study on a particular evening is practicing the strategy of commitment when choosing to avoid the library where most of the student's friends will be studying, thus decreasing the likelihood of cues associated with competing social behavior. Establishing precise stimulus control over an undesirable behavior does not in itself guarantee that the frequency of the behavior will be decreased. My friend John, himself a psychologist, was a heavy smoker who was urged to quit by his physician. When John pleaded that he would be a wreck driving his car without the possibility of smoking, his doctor replied that if he smoked only when in his auto he should be alright. Within weeks John was no longer seen smoking outside his car. The problem, as you might suspect, is that John was now rarely out of his car! Other friends and I were often invited on excursions involving driving.

The direct relevance of stimulus control to cancer therapy has been noted in a study of nausea in chemotherapy

(Bovbjerg, Redd, Jacobsen, Manne, Taylor, Surbone, Crown, Norton, Gilewski, Hudis, Reichman, Kaufman, Currie, and Hakes (1992)[4] done at the Memorial Sloan-Kettering Cancer Center in New York City. The authors note that up to 57 percent of cancer patients come to experience nausea in anticipation of chemotherapy treatment. They note that anticipatory nausea and vomiting are major clinical problems affecting compliance with treatment and quality of life. The Sloan-Kettering study demonstrated that the nausea is a conditioned response to distinctive features of the chemotherapy treatment. Breast cancer chemotherapy outpatients were randomly assigned either to an Experimental Group, which was exposed to a distinctive stimulus before each infusion of chemotherapy, or to a Control Group that was not exposed to the distinctive stimulus. Patients in the Experimental Group reported increased nausea following presentation of this distinctive stimulus in test trials (without chemotherapy) whereas patients in the Control Group did not. This, of course is an example of stimulus control. Through repeated pairings of the distinctive stimulus with the nausea produced by chemotherapy, the stimulus comes to elicit the nausea. As the researchers pointed out, and as I elaborated in the companion editorial (Fantino, 1992), it is possible to use this fact to minimize nausea in chemotherapy administrations. By first presenting the distinctive stimuli without aversive consequences (i.e., without chemotherapy), the ability of the stimuli to be conditioned to subsequent

---

4. An experimental analysis of classically conditioned nausea during cancer chemotherapy. *Psychosomatic Medicine*, 54, 623–637.

nausea (and therefore to subsequently produce anticipatory nausea) will be impaired. For example, one or two administrations of chemotherapy without actual chemotherapy infusions before the actual chemotherapy would render the stimuli associated with chemotherapy as ineffective conditioned stimuli.[5] In other words, future stimulus control will be undermined and significantly less anticipatory nausea should develop.

To summarize, using stimulus control as a self-control strategy involves bringing behavior under control of certain stimuli or situations and then manipulating the likelihood of encountering those stimuli and situations to increase desired behavior or reduce undesired behavior. This effective strategy is best used together with the other self-control strategies discussed in this chapter: commitment, self-reinforcement, and record-keeping. As we use combinations of these strategies and see their effectiveness, we gain a sense of accomplishment and, ultimately, a sense of greater control over our environment and our lives.

Some have criticized behavioral approaches to behavior

---

5. Psychologists refer to this phenomenon as latent inhibition. I discuss it in my editorial, "The Concept of Latent Inhibition and Its Application to Psychosomatic Medicine," referenced above. The basic idea is that "presentations of a stimulus without consequence leads to an impairment in learning about the relationship between that stimulus and some consequence on subsequent exposures. It appears that subjects learn to ignore the stimulus, since it has no predictive value, and are then less likely to pay attention to it when it does have predictive potential" (Fantino, 1992, p.638). In other words, we learn the stimulus or situation is "safe" or irrelevant and tend to stick with this assessment when it no longer applies. Thus, if we get indigestion after eating a meal consisting of a familiar and a novel food, we will attribute our discomfort to the novel food (even though the familiar food or neither food may, in this case, be responsible).

management as ineffective and/or dehumanizing. It is difficult for someone knowledgeable about psychology to take seriously the charge of ineffectiveness. However, a commonly expressed argument among some uninformed critics is that the practice of providing rewards for desirable behavior is a form of bribery that ultimately weakens the desired behavior. Increasingly parents and teachers have turned to external rewards to successfully promote the development of behaviors, including reading, mathematical and social skills, and even creativity. The beauty of this approach becomes evident when the behaviors often become rewarding in themselves and, in turn, lead to other naturally occurring rewards. So, too, in the clinics have rewards been used to provide impaired children with intellectual skills, such as language, and with motor skills, such as walking, both of which then expose the child to a wealth of naturally occurring opportunities for reward. Once activities have been initiated, if they are enjoyable, they will be maintained. Then the external rewards that were useful in initiating the activities may be eliminated, perhaps faded out gradually. Sometimes, of course, such intrinsic motivation may not be enough and external rewards should be maintained. Thus, Eastern European nations are now exposing their economies to the effects of external rewards and punishments found in a free-market economy. Behaviorists have long stressed the naturally rewarding consequences of most behaviors that we engage in, a topic we will return to in a later chapter. For our present purpose, however, the issue of bribery by an external agent such as a teacher, parent, spouse, or employer is irrelevant for at least two reasons. First, we are not advocating bribery in the sense of offering a reward for a future behavior but are advocating following the desired behavior with reward (this distinction between bribery and reinforcement has been made by Karen Pryor in *Don't Shoot the Dog*).[6] Second, and more obvious, here we have not been talking about manipulating someone else's environment to alter their behavior. Instead, we have been talking about manipulating our own environment to control our own behavior (hence, self-control).

A related argument addresses the behavioral strategies of setting up contingencies in our lives, for example constraining TV watching on the basis of completing school assignments. Might not this stifle freedom and creativity? There is no evidence for this. In fact, many developmental psychologists and teachers argue that children, at any rate, *prefer* some limits and constraints on their behavior. No less a creative genius than Leonardo da Vinci said, "Art lives from constraints and dies from freedom." It is self-discipline and self-control that promote accomplishment, creative and otherwise.

Surprising results from a series of ingenious experiments by Professor Allan Neuringer at Reed College in Oregon showed that by rewarding variable responding, subjects could in fact respond with dramatic variability. Neuringer and his students provided subjects with two alternating situations. In one, they could obtain reward only by responding variably. In the other, they were free

---

6. An excellent and highly readable paperback on modifying our behavior is: Pryor, Karen, *Don't Shoot the Dog*, Ringpress Book Ltd., 2002

to respond in any fashion and would obtain reward. How was their responding affected? The situation, which required variability, produced it, but the situation that permitted any sequence of responding produced repetitive, stereotyped responding. In other words, left to their own devices, subjects produced repetitive, stereotypical behavior. Any implications about our everyday lives that are drawn from these results must be speculative. However, they do suggest the possibility that by constraining and structuring our lives in order to achieve our goals, we may be promoting, not inhibiting, freedom. By adopting a laissez faire approach, on the other hand, we may be promoting dull routine in the guise of freedom. Or to paraphrase da Vinci (rather liberally), diversity and creativity of behavior are promoted by constraint and inhibited by freedom.

Of course there is a distinction between freedom and the sense or feel of freedom. For most of us freedom means the sense or belief that we have options among which to choose. What is free and what is not is not always clear to us. Consider the interview given to *Golf World* by golfer John Daly in which he discussed his return to alcohol and gambling addictions. As the New York Times (September 24, 1999) reported:

> John Daly is drinking and gambling again, not sure where it will lead but offering no regrets for losing an endorsement with Callaway Golf that had been his primary source of income. "It's sad, but I think it's great to be free," Daly told *Golf World* magazine in this week's issue.

We would argue that Mr. Daly had traded one set of constraints (not gambling and drinking) for another more confining set (addiction to gambling and alcohol).

I was once confronted with my own sensitivity to environmental constraints while teaching my class on learning and motivation. At that time, I was a pipe smoker and smoking was permitted at UCSD. Midway through the course, five students came up to me with a graph showing how much time I spent during each class smoking my pipe. I smoked during about 10 percent of the class time until the third week (noted by an arrow on the graph) whereupon the frequency of my pipe smoking increased steadily to a level of about 30 percent. It turned out that beginning in that third week, these five students smiled and sat in rapt attention whenever I was smoking my pipe. They wanted to learn if this social reinforcement would increase my pipe smoking. They were convinced that it had and wanted to share with me this graphic affirmation of the reinforcement principles we had been discussing in the course. But, instead of reacting with pleasure at this affirmation, my initial reaction was annoyance. I resented the fact that my behavior was so readily manipulated!

As I mentioned previously, some have suggested that the use of rewards and the manipulation of environmental controls to alter behavior is somehow dehumanizing. As my pipe-smoking example illustrates, we sometimes resent the implication that our behavior is sensitive to external rewards and punishments (rather than driven entirely by free will). Like it or not, our behavior is influenced by the external world. The real choice is between allowing our behavior to be manipulated while remaining ignorant of its causes or in understanding and seizing control of the determinants of our behavior. The ultimate triumph of a humane approach to behavior may be in the successful manipulation of the behavioral strategies now at our disposal to help us better achieve our goals. The strategies for self-control discussed in these pages have been proven effective in countless studies. They are at our disposal as tools for helping us meet our objectives in life. I know that they have helped me in mine.

tips for living

SELF-CONTROL IS A CHOICE between an immediate small reward and a delayed larger reward. Learn behavioral strategies to break a preoccupation with short-term gains by rearranging your own consequences whenever possible.

REVIEW BEHAVIORAL RESEARCH to understand the conditions that cause us to behave either impulsively or to demonstrate self-control. Then take informed steps for altering your impulsivity.

CHANGE AVAILABILITY OF YOUR TEMPTATIONS. For example, if you can't resist Ben & Jerry's double-fudge, caramel ice cream, don't buy it.

WHENEVER POSSIBLE, COMMIT IN ADVANCE, especially when unpleasant events are involved. For example, schedule your annual physical far in advance when taking that healthy option appears more inviting.

SCHEDULE SELF-REINFORCEMENT. Complete a task that you need to finish, but don't necessarily want to do, then follow it with a rewarding activity such as reading or taking a walk.

In this way you rearrange the relationship between formerly competing activities to become complementary activities.

MAINTAIN A RECORD OF YOUR ACHIEVEMENTS: number of miles walked, pages written, calls made, safety measures taken, any measure that marks your success. Record-keeping makes achievement salient and serves as an excellent tool for self-control.

IF POSSIBLE, USE THE PROCESS OF FADING, or gradually reducing a bad habit over time. Record-keeping aids this process so that you can't delude yourself over, say, how many cigarettes you are really smoking per day.

THE MERE ACT OF RECORD-KEEPING will often greatly enable you to overcome a bad habit or improve a good one even in the absence of additional behavioral interventions.

VISUALIZE YOUR LONG-TERM GOALS when facing tempting situations.

EXERCISE STIMULUS CONTROL. Behaviors are more likely to be repeated in situations and locales where they have been enjoyed in the past.

MAKE THE DECISION to examine and understand the stimuli and consequences that influence your behavior and take control of those elements, rather than impulsively reacting.

know thyself

What is a successful, satisfying life? Collect answers from a number of people and you will find great disagreement on specifics but fairly good consensus on the broader outlines of the answer. A successful and satisfying life is one in which we find a fair degree of emotional contentment and a sense of having succeeded in attaining some of our goals. The specific goals may vary markedly from individual to individual as will the means for attaining them. Moreover, a degree of accomplishment that satisfies one person may be held far short of the mark by another.

The first step toward doing better is knowing what we want, and because this is so important, I'd like to briefly discuss one last strategy that can help in defining our goals and rearranging our lives to achieve them.

Some individuals will never feel that they have achieved their goals in life because their goals are either unrealistic or because they are not specified. Unrealistic goals include those over which we have little direct control (such as winning a major payoff in a lottery or seeing your child become a successful brain surgeon). If we sat down and thought about our goals and tried to develop a realistic

plan for achieving them, we could at least minimize the
setting of unrealistic goals, since we would become aware
that we have no realistic plans for arriving at them. This
exercise would also prevent us from drifting aimlessly
from day to day with goals unspecified. The expression
seize the day is not merely a prescription for living one
day at a time. It stresses making the most of each day.
Whether we are talking about making the most of today
or making the most of the next five years, we need to
know what we want to achieve if we are to have a chance
of doing so.

As strange as it seems to some of us, many individuals
aren't sure of what they want from life, making it difficult
to plan effectively, but most of us at least have a good
sense of what we like to do and even what we would like
to be doing in five years' time. How would we determine
what a specific individual likes to do? We would observe
his or her behavior. Ideally, these observations would
occur with minimal constraints so that the individual is
free, at least for a time, to act in any fashion. In this ideal
period of observation we would measure the activities
engaged in and the amount of time spent in each. From
this we could construct what is known technically as a
reinforcement hierarchy with behaviors at the top being
those that are performed with the greatest likelihood,
given the chance; those behaviors at the bottom of the
hierarchy are those rarely engaged in even when the
opportunity to do so is unlimited. Once a reliable reinforcement hierarchy is constructed, it can be shown to
have important properties for behavior change.

May we generate our own reinforcement hierarchy in a

relatively nonrigorous manner simply by reflecting on our own behavior? Yes, and we can probably improve on its accuracy by consulting friends or family members for their opinion of what we enjoy doing. In this way, I've constructed my own reinforcement hierarchy (which probably isn't so dramatically different from one that would be generated properly, in a more rigorous but cumbersome long-term study). I'll share it with you, to give you perhaps a clearer idea of what I mean by a reinforcement hierarchy. Below I list some representative activities from those I would engage in with greatest likelihood at the top, down to those I would prefer to rarely or never engage in, at the bottom. The list is necessarily abbreviated: listing every activity we humans engage in would take several pages and some are too personal to include in a published list. So here is my partial but representative reinforcement hierarchy:

1. Conducting psychological research
2. Eating
3. Attending theater (with family)
4. Hiking/walking
5. Reading novels
6. Listening to classical music
7. Attending movies (with family)
8. Teaching
9. Reading newspaper
10. Reviewing scientific articles
11. Cooking
12. Shopping
13. Watching TV shows
14. Doing dishes
15. Taking out garbage
16. Washing our car

Obviously, even this partial list is somewhat oversimplified. For me, any of the activities would move up the hierarchy if done with family members. Second, the enjoyability of attending the theater, reading a book, or watching TV will depend upon the particular selection. I am assuming here an above-average play, novel, or TV show. Similarly, hiking can be spectacular: for example, the walk Stephanie and I took, the day before I wrote these words, up to the summit of Mount Cargill, overlooking Dunedin, New Zealand, where we were spending five months would rate at the top of my hierarchy. On the other hand, a more mundane walk around the neighborhood would be ranked much lower. My placement is something of a composite of many different types of walk.

There are more important senses in which this hierarchy is oversimplified. It suggests that, given free opportunity, I would spend relatively little time shopping for food and cooking it, yet eating is very high on the hierarchy. How can I have the food I love without buying and cooking it? And how can I conduct psychological research (the activity at the top of my hierarchy) effectively without obtaining the proper background (from activities such as reading scientific articles, ranked below the middle)? The answer to this question will tell us quite a bit about changing our behavior. A second sense in which this hierarchy is oversimplified involves the placement of an activity such as eating on the hierarchy without specifying my internal state (have I just eaten or have I not eaten yet today?). This too is a critical aspect of behavior change. Before we discuss these two questions and, more generally, indicate how appreciation and manipulation of the activities making up our individual hierarchies may help us to attain our goals, I return briefly to the question, "What are the activities we enjoy doing?"

The decision on activities you want to do is necessarily a personal one. However, the very exercise of constructing your reinforcement hierarchy may help you to order your priorities. Once you have generated a hierarchy, you may want to show it to those who know you and see if your view of your preferred behavior is consistent with others' views. You may be in for a surprise!

Now that you have your reinforcement hierarchy, you are ready to enlist its aid, and to see how this is done, we return to the two issues raised above.

We noted that engaging in preferred activities such as (for me) doing research or eating, often depends on successful completion of less preferred activities. Some of us, for example, would spend less time at our job, if we had the opportunity, were it not for the fact that the money earned there enables us to engage in more rewarding activities, namely those higher on the reinforcement hierarchy. Thus if my occupation were working at a car wash (instead of conducting psychological research), I would spend large amounts of my time washing cars, an activity that I would almost never engage in given my unconstrained reinforcement hierarchy. In other words, my performance of a non-preferred activity will increase in frequency if it makes possible the opportunity to engage in a more preferred activity. This is known as reinforcement, a concept (and its usefulness) developed in great detail by B. F. Skinner. The notion of a reinforcement hierarchy was developed by David Premack who also promulgated a principle that sometime bears his name (The Premack Principle). Recall that for all of us there is a reinforcement hierarchy: those behaviors at the top being those we would perform with greatest likelihood, given the chance; those behaviors at the bottom being those in which we would rarely engage. The Premack Principle states that for a given individual, any activity in the hierarchy may reinforce (make more likely) any response below it and may itself be reinforced by any response above it. Thus, for me, the opportunity to eat my brown rice and vegetables when hungry will strengthen the likelihood that I will shop for these goods and cook them (though otherwise I would rather be reading or hiking than shopping or cooking). And, the opportunity to cook may, in turn, strengthen the activities lower in the hierarchy; for instance, I may find it necessary to put out the garbage or do the dishes before I can cook comfortably.

Evidence for this principle is extensive. Consider an early example in which children were given the choice of eating candy or operating a pinball machine. Premack found that children who preferred eating candy would increase their frequency of pinball playing if it were required to obtain candy. Similarly, children who preferred playing the pinball machine would increase their intake of candy if eating candy were required to get the opportunity to play the pinball machine. Moreover, these relations could be *reversed*. For example, when a child who preferred the pinball machine became sufficiently hungry, candy would come to reinforce pinball playing. In general, then, a shift in the relative probabilities of engaging in particular activities brings with it a shift in the reinforcing effectiveness of these activities.

Laymen who are intuitively wise in the ways of behavior have long applied the Premack Principle. When a parent requires a child to clean up his room before he can watch his favorite TV program, he is employing the principle.

On the other hand, he is *not* doing so if he tells the child he can watch the program provided that he cleans his room afterwards. The Premack Principle has had successful application in the classroom as well as the home. For example, pupils' writing abilities have been significantly increased by allowing the students the opportunity to play after successfully completing their assignments. In one study, the opportunity to engage in a highly preferred academic subject actually served to improve performance in a less-preferred subject.

By considering your own reinforcement hierarchy within the context of your long-term goals you may find ways of increasing the likelihood of engaging in activities that permit a more desirable ultimate distribution of activities. Going on a cruise to the South Pacific may be high on someone's list but not possible owing to financial or time constraints. But, the opportunity to go on the cruise should strengthen the activities necessary to obtain it. Confronting your hierarchy may help you appreciate not only what you want to do but also how you might go about it.

The second issue concerns our internal states and deprivations. While eating is high on my reinforcement hierarchy usually, it certainly is not immediately after a satisfying repast. In fact, though perhaps less obvious, the likelihood of engaging in any of our usual activities is influenced by how much we have engaged in them recently. This fact gives us greater flexibility in arranging our activities. By depriving ourselves of the opportunity to engage in an activity for a while, we can then use that same activity to strengthen the performance of an activity that we seek to increase. For example, by restricting television viewing, that activity may be used as a reward (or strengthener) of another behavior that we want to increase (because by doing so we will move closer to achieving an intermediate-term or long-term goal).

However, there may be pitfalls. A common one that is important enough to discuss involves what behavioral economists would call the *possible substitutability of activities*. For example, you may institute the TV contingency and find that you don't increase the desired activity, but merely forgo TV watching as well. It may be that other reinforcing activities substitute for the restricted activity (TV watching). In that case, of course, we would include these activities in the contingency as well. (To take an extreme example, depriving an individual of drinking Coca-Cola should have little effect on behavior if Pepsi and other colas are freely available.)

Studies have shown that application of the Premack Principle may be extremely effective in strengthening behavior low on the reinforcement hierarchy. Once the routine of following a less desired activity with a preferred activity is established, the two will come to represent complementary, not competing, activities. It is often the case that once instituted, the behavior change may become relatively permanent even after the contingency is removed. One may come to enjoy some of the less preferred activity more as he or she becomes more proficient at it.

When we are dealing with our own reinforcement hierarchy, we decide on the manipulation and contingencies. Unfortunately, this means we have to trust ourselves to enforce the contingency, but we have means at our disposal. In particular, this is where we may bring to bear the strategies for self-control discussed in Chapter 5: commitment; self-reinforcement; record-keeping; stimulus control. For simplicity's sake, let's assume an adult has placed television high on her reinforcement hierarchy and this adult is struggling to complete a correspondence school course in tax accounting. She might divide a week's assignment into five parts and set up a contingency between completing one part of the assignment each weekday evening and watching TV subsequently for up to two hours. (If the preferred shows are on early, they can be taped). It will be up to this adult to self-monitor her performance. Note that setting up a contingency between completing the assignment and watching TV already incorporates two of the four self-control strategies we discussed: self-reinforcement, since assignment completion will be followed by TV watching; and record-keeping, since the assignment completion will be noted. Commitment may already be involved in a global sense since the correspondence course has probably already been paid. If convenient, it would be desirable to employ a commitment strategy on a nightly basis, for example, if there is a roommate present who will agree to help with arranging for the availability of the TV. Even a Post-it™ on the TV itself asking, "Did you complete your assignment?" may help. Finally, the principle of stimulus control should be employed much as was suggested in discussing study behavior in Chapter 5. Do the assignment in an area reserved for working on the assignment so that the cues in that area come to be associated with and promote such work.

There will also be times when it is the activity at the top of the hierarchy that you would like to increase. Here the Premack Principle has no obvious application since there is no more-valued alternative to serve as a reinforcer. The principles of self-control are still available to help in this instance.

A final suggestion: when trying to eliminate or reduce a particular behavior, it is generally helpful to substitute another, more desirable behavior. In this way, a new (desirable) action becomes associated with (conditioned to) the stimuli that up to now have set the occasion for engaging in the old (undesirable) action. In the case of someone who wants to reduce caffeine intake, this could involve change as simple as switching to decaffeinated coffee or herbal tea. In the case of a dieter accustomed to a slice of apple pie with his twenty-minute afternoon break, this could involve a brisk twenty-minute walk, which will not only burn calories instead of adding them but will also serve as a short-term appetite suppressant and will soon become enjoyable in its own right. The substitute activity will make the behavior change easier to accomplish and maintain since it will disrupt the old (and perhaps strong) association between the situation and the undesirable behavior that used to occur in it.

Ultimately, of course, the decision to follow through on your good intentions is yours. These techniques may be helpful in clarifying your goals and in helping to achieve them. I've found these principles useful and I hope you do too.

☺ tips for living ———————————————

OBSERVE YOUR BEHAVIOR to create a reinforcement hierarchy, a list of the activities that you most enjoy with number one being your favorite pastime. Record the amount of time that you tend to spend on each activity during a few days or a week. Ask a friend or relative for feedback on the accuracy of your hierarchy list.

EMPLOY THE PREMACK PRINCIPLE of reinforcing a lesser desired activity with a more desirable activity. In this way, you can complete some of the less enjoyable activities that are necessary for achieving a goal.

USE THE BEHAVIORAL APPROACH OF DEPRIVATION to move closer to reaching an intermediate or long-term goal. By depriving yourself from engaging in an enjoyed activity for a certain amount of time, you can strengthen the performance of another activity that you wish to increase. For example, you cannot watch television until you walk one mile on the treadmill. Be aware of the pitfalls of substitutability of activities. In other words, don't decide not to walk and not to watch television, but just to sit on the sofa with a beer and the sports section instead.

ENFORCE YOUR OWN CONTINGENCIES or rules for reward using the self-control strategies mentioned previously: self-reinforcement, record keeping, commitment, and stimulus control. For example, don't go to Starbucks if you're trying to reduce your caffeine intake.

WHEN TRYING TO eliminate or reduce a behavior, replace it with another more desirable behavior. This will disrupt the behavior you are attempting to eliminate or reduce. Often, the newer, healthier behavior will become more rewarding than the original habit that it replaced.

WRITE DOWN YOUR GOALS for the next five years as a trigger to get yourself started and, above all, enjoy your life!

additional five-year plans

I am enjoying what I hope will be a full fourth set of five years. The biggest emotional problem I now face is maintaining the new and richer perspective on life that my ongoing brush with death has given me. Recall that this experience has given me an attitude conducive to obtaining the maximum enjoyment in life. It has permitted me to better appreciate those aspects of my life and my environment that are always present, always there to please if I would only consider them. It has permitted me to fully enjoy successes and the pleasant aspects of my life and to ignore or minimize the impact of failures and the less pleasant aspects. But as the years go on and my health remains precarious but stable, it is sometimes difficult to maintain this constructive outlook. Rather, I find that the potentially annoying, frustrating, and sometimes downright dismal facets of life can bother me as much as they ever did. So to some extent the magic has worn off, but usually not for long.

When I catch myself becoming overly upset about something or when I realize that I am not appreciating something worthwhile (if only flowers in bloom or the smile of my daughters), then I readjust. Whether I have a few years left or another thirty, that's still precious little time. Why waste it by dwelling on the negative or by failing to appreciate the activities I enjoy and the sensations that fill my existence?

For the time being, I have a fourth five-year plan of activities I plan to engage in and accomplishments to which I aspire. Achieving goals is difficult in the best case, but it is almost hopeless if you are not clear on the goals in the first place. So begin by deciding what you would like to accomplish over the next five years. Make sure that these goals are compatible with one another. If not, eliminate the less important of the incompatible ones. Make certain you can realistically get from your present situation to the situations you would prefer to find yourself in during the next five years. Obviously some attention must be given to even longer-term planning (retirement and a toddler's college education fifteen years away must not be lost sight of); however, the emphasis should be on steps to be taken now and on enjoying the fruits of their successful implementation.

My own plan for my second five years was simple, and since personal own plans are seldom of great interest to others I will comment on them only very briefly. One objective was to write this book. If you are reading it now, I have succeeded in that objective. Whether the book achieves its goals of providing guidance on how to better deal with stressful medical news and, more generally, how to use behavioral principles to enrich life, is for you to tell me. A second objective was to attend an annual "macrobiotic camp" at the Mendocino Woodlands, near stunningly beautiful Mendocino, California. Our family had attended this week-long vacation paradise twice in the prior five years and succeeded in doing so again in 1995. At this camp a few dozen families and individuals get together for a week of workshops and social interaction in an idyllic redwood forest setting. Workshops and activities include yoga, tai-chi, cooking, health, nutrition, environmental issues, art, life styles, and activities for children. People from different backgrounds and occupations come together for interesting discussions. Three delicious macrobiotic meals are provided daily and the area offers marvelous hikes, vistas, wildlife, and flora. We have felt immensely enriched by participating. Other accomplishments in that second set of five years included the following: completing several research projects in my psychology laboratory and supervising my six graduate students toward obtaining their Ph.D.; continuing to spend time with my family, including attending concerts, theater, and opera together, and traveling; now that the children were old enough, walking the Milford Track in the Fiordland of the South Island of New Zealand, a four-day, thirty-four-mile backpacking trip, said to be the world's most beautiful walk; reading a novel a week; remaining active leading hikes and camping trips with the Focus on Youth section of the Sierra Club. Of course there were many other things I would have liked to accomplish, but perhaps I would have another five years to work on those.

What are my prospects and why am I doing as well as I have been? I don't know. On the negative side, beginning in mid-1991, several changes occurred. First I noticed, after two and a half years on the macrobiotic diet, that my sex drive was regaining much of its lost momentum. Also my gradual weight loss ended and I gained four pounds. We were in Australia at the time and I wondered if my body's adjustment to the diet, particularly the suggestion of increased hormonal activity, was also correlated with an increase in my PSA blood test score. Sure enough when we returned, and for the next several years, my PSA count gradually increased above the normal range. Ultimately, it was necessary to resort to hormonal therapy and chemotherapy on which I am periodically maintained.

On the positive side, I feel great, am enjoying life, and have no symptoms other than the side effects of the various treatments. So, whatever the ultimate outcome, I consider myself a fortunate individual.

Am I continuing with my yoga exercises and my macrobiotic diet in the hope of maintaining a vigorous immune system? As seriously and rigorously as ever! I continue to enjoy both. I could offer only anecdotal evidence in support of their effectiveness, but given my own experience I am not about to risk giving up either. If this were only an academic question I would, of course, conduct a little experiment with myself. I would give up the diet (or the Yoga) for a few months and note how this affected my perceived well-being, including susceptibility to colds and, of course, my blood test. Then, I would resume the diet (or the Yoga) for a time, note any changes, and give the other up for a few months. In this way, I might develop a good idea on the effectiveness of each, though being my only subject, any conclusions would be tentative. Assuming my intuition that both Kundalini Yoga and

macrobiotics are helping my condition, this is what I
might find: eliminating either, and especially deleting
both, would cause me to feel less fit, more susceptible to
illness, and elevate my PSA test scores. The satisfaction I
could gain in terms of pride in confirming my intuition in
this manner would be more than overwhelmed by the
potential havoc it would have wrought. So, I leave it to a
healthy reader to try these changes in life style and see
how it helps subjective fitness. Let me know!

I do know that I have met many individuals who claim
that their health and fitness have been improved by either
Kundalini Yoga or by a macrobiotic diet. Although these
individuals are as sincerely convinced as I am that these
changes in life style have contributed to their improved
sense of well-being, there is no way to be certain. Perhaps
the most impressive testimonial I encountered was one I
heard quite by accident. Stephanie was talking to our
daughter Marin's grade-school teacher some years ago and
happened to mention that she and I were off to lunch
that afternoon in San Diego. When the teacher asked
where, Stephanie replied "Grain Country; it's a natural-
foods store and restaurant that we go to once a week to
shop and have lunch."[7] The teacher replied: "Oh, Grain
Country! My father eats there all the time." She then pro-
ceeded to tell Stephanie about her dad's medical
condition. He, too, had prostate cancer, which became
very advanced. Eventually he exhausted all treatment

---

7. Unfortunately, this fine store, the only macrobiotic restaurant in the San Diego
area, closed in 1991. Stephanie and I greatly enjoyed these weekly excursions and
the people we encountered there.

options including aggressive hormone therapy. His cancer spread to his bones and he was given just months to live. At this point, he tried a macrobiotic diet. He improved and now, several years later, appears fine. This was certainly encouraging news!

Somehow, hearing about an unexpected cure from someone you know is more impressive than reading about one in a newspaper or book, perhaps because you can relate to it so much more directly. Whether or not someone else's circumstances are comparable to your own, however, is something that is always difficult to evaluate. When we are experimenting with our own health, we are really unique subjects and what might be best for one person may not necessarily be best for another. Thus, my experience with prostate cancer, and whether or not I ultimately succumb to it, is not necessarily an experience that has relevance for others with prostate cancer. What I hoped to convey were not the specifics for a plan to combat prostate cancer, rather a general behavioral attitudinal and emotional strategy for coping with life and the trials it invariably entails.

When faced with the prospect of serious illness or loss, the most important lesson I would like to convey based on my own experience is to try and take control of the situation. One can investigate, plan, and act to improve the situation, but why wait until the prospect of serious illness? More generally, we can act now to shape our life to be more fulfilling. Don't wait, as I did, for an incurable illness to prod you into action.

I said earlier that I wished I had made my changes in life style years before I did. "If I knew then what I know

now..." I would have been enjoying my Kundalini exercises and my macrobiotic diet all my life, and I would have rearranged my professional and personal life so as to better direct my actions toward the achievement of my most essential goals.

While on the subject of *what might have been,* I will share one last experience which might help serve as a useful lesson. The year before my cancer was diagnosed I had a routine physical examination, my annual check-up. During this visit, my doctor did not perform a rectal examination. Knowing that this was advised annually,[8] I almost spoke up and requested one. Timidity won out, however, and I didn't. Would an examination then have made a difference; that is, would my cancer have been detected a year earlier? And, if so, would it have then been confined to the prostate and, therefore, curable? I'll never know the answers to these questions. Nor is there any point to dwelling on them; but I do urge others to be less timid about requesting rectal examinations. More generally, become better aware of preventative health measures and be more aggressive in pursuing them. If you are fortunate enough to be in good health and feeling fit, do what you can to protect your privileged status. Whatever you do, don't take good fortune for granted.

Whether we feel fortune is smiling on us, as I did walking along a beach in Kauai at the start of my story, or

---

8. In fact a friend years before had impressed upon me the importance of annual rectal examinations to detect prostate cancer. I knew this was good advice. Yet being forewarned was apparently not enough in my case!

whether we are having trouble coping with life's basic demands, we can do better.

Always remember that the very phrase *self-control* makes it clear who is in control and that is why I've written this little book. I want to share my conviction that however bleak and seemingly hopeless a turn our lives may take, we still have control over our actions. Simply by exercising this control, we may feel more comfortable with our situation. We may even improve it to the point that, while we can't necessarily alter the outcome, we can at least make the situation less bleak and more hopeful. We owe it to our family and friends, and above all ourselves, to do no less.

Why not decide to take more effective control of our lives now, rather than wait until tragedy strikes, as I did? The mere act of writing down your goals for the next five years can be an exciting spur to constructive change, but you can't do that while you are reading this. So, I'll stop now. Good Luck!

tips for living

WORK TO MAINTAIN an attitude conducive to gaining the maximum joy from your life. Do so by fully enjoying even small successes and ignoring or minimizing failures.

CLARIFY YOUR GOALS for the next five years. If you don't know the nature of your goals, you can't set about achieving them. Write your goals down and the specific steps you have for meeting those goals. This will help you determine if your goals are unrealistic or if they compete with one another.

The less control you have over achieving a goal, the less realistic that goal is; for example, one has little to no control over the goal of winning the lottery. If the means for reaching goals conflict, eliminate the less important goals and revisit them after you have achieved your priority goal.

DO THE NECESSARY PLANNING for long-term goals, but set up the rewards/contingencies so that you actually enjoy completing the steps required for achieving the goal.

IMPLEMENT BEHAVIORAL PRINCIPLES of reward and reinforcement to continually enrich your life experience. Participate in varied activities, learning opportunities, and in the maintenance of your own health.

CONTINUE, CONTINUE, CONTINUE practicing and honing the skills of behavioral strategies for positively coping. Often this simply means taking as much control as is feasibly possible of any situation. That control can start with investigating, planning, and acting immediately to improve current conditions.

SHAPE YOUR LIFE to be a more fulfilling one. Don't wait to be confronted by tragedy before you attempt to make positive changes. Rearrange your professional and personal life to direct your actions toward the achievement of your most essential goals.

DON'T BE TIMID. Ask questions. Challenge assumptions. Become better aware of preventative health measures and aggressively pursue them. Never take good fortune for granted.

DETERMINE WHAT YOU REALLY WANT, which is the first critical step in defining and then achieving your goals.

about the author

Edmund Fantino, Ph.D., is a psychologist, author and researcher in decision making. He studies choice in humans and pigeons, including nonoptimal and illogical decisions. He is Professor of Psychology and of the Neurosciences Group at the University of California, San Diego (UCSD). His books include The Experimental Analysis of Behavior: A Biological Perspective (with C.A. Logan).

about ADI

Aubrey Daniels International (ADI) helps the world's leading businesses use the scientifically proven laws of human behavior to promote workplace practices vital to long-term success. By developing strategies that reinforce critical work behaviors, ADI enables clients such as DaimlerChrysler Financial Services, Dollar General, and Blue Cross and Blue Shield, achieve and sustain consistently high levels of performance, building profitable habits™ within their organizations. ADI is led by Dr. Aubrey C. Daniels, the world's foremost authority on behavioral science in the workplace. Headquartered in Atlanta, the firm was founded in 1978.

other ADI titles

Measure of a Leader

Aubrey C. Daniels
James E. Daniels

Ethics At Work

Alice Darnell Lattal
Ralph W. Clark

Other People's Habits

Aubrey C. Daniels

Bringing Out the Best In People

Aubrey C. Daniels

Performance Management: Changing Behavior That Drives Organizational Effectiveness *(4th edition)*

Aubrey C. Daniels
James E. Daniels

Precision Selling

Joseph S. Laipple

You Can't Apologize to a Dawg!

Tucker Childers

For more information call **1.800.223.6191**
or visit our Web site **www.aubreydaniels.com**

register your book

Register your book and receive exclusive reader benefits. Visit the Web site below and click on the "Register Your Book" link at the top of the page. Registration is free.

www.pmanagementpubs.com

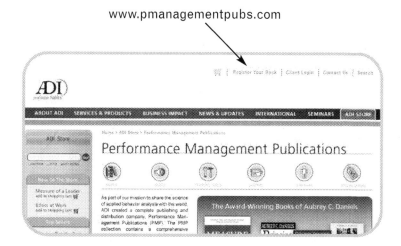